King Leopold's Congo and the "Scramble for Africa"

A Short History with Documents

King Leopold's Congo and the "Scramble for Africa"

A Short History with Documents

Michael A. Rutz

Hackett Publishing Company, Inc.
Indianapolis/Cambridge

Copyright © 2018 by Hackett Publishing Company, Inc.

21 20 19 18   1 2 3 4 5 6 7

For further information, please address
    Hackett Publishing Company, Inc.
    P.O. Box 44937
    Indianapolis, Indiana 46244-0937

    www.hackettpublishing.com

Cover design by Rick Todhunter
Interior design by Laura Clark
Composition by Aptara, Inc.

Library of Congress Cataloging-in-Publication Data
Names: Rutz, Michael A., 1970– author.
Title: King Leopold's Congo and the "scramble for Africa" : a short history
  with documents / Michael A. Rutz.
Other titles: Passages (Indianapolis, Ind.)
Description: Indianapolis ; Cambridge : Hackett Publishing Company, Inc.,
  2018. | Series: Passages | Includes bibliographical references and index.
Identifiers: LCCN 2017034198 | ISBN 9781624666568 (pbk.) | ISBN
9781624666575 (cloth)
Subjects: LCSH: Congo (Democratic Republic)—History. | Congo
(Democratic Republic)—History—Sources. | Congo (Democratic
Republic)—Colonial influence.
Classification: LCC DT652 .R88 2018 | DDC 967.5102—dc23
LC record available at https://lccn.loc.gov/2017034198

∞

CONTENTS

ACKNOWLEDGMENTS

I wish to thank Rick Todhunter, Laura Clark, and the entire production team at Hackett Publishing for providing me with the opportunity to contribute this volume to the Passages: Key Moments in History series. Their efforts have made writing this book an enjoyable experience every step of the way. Thanks to the publisher's readers, and to friends and colleagues whose advice and suggestions have made this a better book at the end than it was at the start. I am especially grateful to Tim Parsons who introduced me to African history during graduate school, an unexpected turn in my studies that has proved to be immensely rewarding over more than a decade of teaching African history to students at the University of Wisconsin Oshkosh. I also want to thank Steve Hause, who taught me much about Europe during the age of imperialism, taught me more about how to be a first-rate historian, and who reviewed my translations of documents in this book from the original French. Stuart Brinkman, one of our many talented UW Oshkosh students, created the map for this volume. Finally, I am forever grateful to my wife, Heather McCombs, for her patience, encouragement, and support. She is a woman of great creative talent, a skilled writer, and a true believer in the spirit of fairness and justice. The story of the Congo compels us to think hard about past and present issues of fairness and justice. For this reason, and many others, this book is dedicated to Heather.

CHRONOLOGY

1200–1300s	Formation and rise of the Kongo Kingdom in the region of present-day western Congo and northern Angola.
1482–84	Portuguese explorer Diogo Cão establishes first European contact with and presence in the Congo region.
1509–40s	Manikongo Mvemba a Nzinga, also known as King Afonso I, rules the Kongo. He adopts some elements of European culture (Christianity and "science"), but also critiques the negative impact of Portuguese commerce and the slave trade on his kingdom.
16th–18th centuries	The transatlantic slave trade expands and continues on the African coast, including the Congo.
1865	Leopold II becomes king of the Belgians.
1874–77	Henry Morton Stanley is the first European to cross the African continent from east to west via the Congo River.
1876	King Leopold II of Belgium holds the Brussels Geographic Congress and establishes the International African Association, initiating his plan to colonize the Congo region.
1879	Leopold establishes the International Congo Society (ICS) with the explicit aim of establishing an economic and colonial presence in the Congo.
1879–84	Leopold commissions Stanley to revisit the Congo, develop the region, and establish treaties with rulers along the Congo River in the name of the king and the ICS.

x   *Chronology*

1880   Pierre Savorgnan de Brazza establishes French claim to the northern bank of the Congo River.

1884–85   The Berlin Conference accepts Leopold's claim to the regions south of the Congo River, and recognizes sovereignty of the ICS over those territories. Leopold establishes the Congo Free State as the colonial government in the Congo, under his personal rule.

1884–87   Tippu Tip claims authority over the eastern Congo region of the Lualaba River in the name of the Sultan of Zanzibar.

1887   John Boyd Dunlop develops the first practical pneumatic rubber tire, setting off the international rubber boom and the exploitation of rubber in the Congo Free State.

1887–92   Tippu Tip allies with the Congo Free State, and is appointed governor of Stanley Falls District in the eastern Congo.

1890   George Washington Williams publishes *An Open Letter to His Serene Majesty, Leopold II, King of the Belgians and Sovereign of the Independent State of Congo*.

1891–92   The Congo Free State expands southward into the region of Katanga.

1892–94   Congo-Arab war, a military campaign against Swahili slave traders, brings the eastern Congo region fully under Congo Free State control.

1900   E. D. Morel begins publishing articles detailing accusations of forced labor and abuses in the Congo Free State.

1904   E. D. Morel, Roger Casement, and Dr. Henry Gratton Guinness found the Congo Reform Association. Casement's government report on abuses in the Congo is published.

1906	King Leopold II sends the Commission of Inquiry to investigate administration of the Congo Free State. The commission report confirms existence of abuses and forced labor.
1908	Leopold cedes his personal control over the Congo Free State, and the Belgian government officially annexes the colony.
1908–60	The Belgian government rules the Congo territory as a colony.
1959–60	Nationalist protests force Belgium to grant independence to the Congo. A new government is formed under the leadership of President Joseph Kasavubu and Prime Minister Patrice Lumumba. Congolese soldiers revolt in southern province of Katanga.
1961	Patrice Lumumba is deposed and assassinated in Katanga, with likely involvement of the Belgian and U.S. governments.
1965	The Kasavubu government is ousted in a coup led by Joseph-Désiré Mobutu.
1971–72	Mobutu renames the country the Republic of Zaire, and changes his name to Mobutu Sese Seko.
1972–97	Mobutu Sese Seko rules Zaire as a dictator, and exploits the resources of the country for his personal gain.
1997	Tutsi and anti-Mobutu rebels, aided by Rwanda, capture the capital city of Kinshasa in the First Congo War. Mobutu's government is replaced by a new regime led by President Laurent-Désiré Kabila. The country is renamed Democratic Republic of the Congo.

1998–2003   Second Congo War, fought primarily in the eastern Congo, develops out of the unstable aftermath of the overthrow of Mobutu. Involving troops from nine African nations and nearly twenty armed rebel groups, the conflict results in nearly 5.5 million deaths.

PREFACE

During the fall of 1906, New Yorkers flocked to the Zoological Park in the Bronx in record numbers. The attraction that drew the attention of such large crowds was not a new animal exhibit, but a young man from Central Africa named Ota Benga put on display with chimpanzees and orangutans in the primate house. In an article headlined "Bushman Shares a Cage with Bronx Park Apes," *The New York Times* described crowds of 300–500 people gathering to watch "the little black man amuse himself."[1] Ota Benga's exhibition at the primate house stirred some controversy. Prominent African American ministers protested against it to zoo administrators and to the mayor of New York City. At least one observer of the exhibit told the *Times* flat out that there was "something about it that I don't like." However, for the vast majority of the more than 200,000 people who visited the zoo throughout the month of September 1906, the display of an African man in a cage with apes represented a fascinating mix of entertainment and educational spectacle. Nor was the exhibit uncommon for the time. Ota Benga had appeared previously in a "native exhibit" at the 1904 St. Louis World's Fair, and "human zoo" exhibits were common at the time in European cities like Paris, Berlin, London, Milan, and Brussels.

The popularity of these exhibits reflected the general attitudes of cultural and racial superiority that prevailed in the West during the age of imperialism. The Bronx Zoo's director, William Temple Hornaday, defended the display as an important "ethnological exhibit," and the *Times* argued that the primate cage, not the schoolroom, was the proper place for Ota Benga since "the idea that men are all much alike except as they have had or lacked opportunities for getting an education of books is now far out of date." Educated elites and ordinary people throughout the West simply assumed that Ota Benga's inferiority, and his status as a subject of scientific study, was a truth evidenced by what they saw as the technological, economic, and cultural supremacy of their civilization

---

1. "Bushman Shares a Cage with Bronx Park Apes," *The New York Times*, September 9, 1906; also cited in Pamela Newkirk, "The Man Who Was Caged in a Zoo," *The Guardian*, June 3, 2015.

compared to his. Following the end of the exhibit, Benga was released to the care of Reverend James H. Gordon, an African American minister who arranged for some basic schooling and eventually settled Benga with a family in Lynchburg, Virginia. He learned English and worked for a time in a tobacco factory. In March 1916, reportedly in despair over not being able to return during World War I to his native Africa, Ota Benga took his own life.

Ota Benga's life story began in his home region of the Kasai River in what was at the turn of the twentieth century the Congo Free State, a territory of 900,000 square miles in central Africa under the personal rule of King Leopold II of Belgium. He was brought to America by Samuel Verner, a missionary and explorer who was contracted by the organizers of the St. Louis World's Fair to lead an expedition to Africa to acquire "natives" to exhibit at the fair. Verner chose the Congo because of a personal friendship with the king, who promised Verner passage and assistance with his "diplomatic mission." Although Verner reported that Ota Benga willingly joined him, it is more likely that Verner acquired him from a well-known slave market in the area of the town of Bassongo. It may seem beyond belief that just over a century ago a man could be taken from his homeland and put on display alongside animals in a zoo in the name of science and education. However, during the age of imperialism attitudes about science, race, and history across elite and popular culture provided ready justifications for the exhibition of Ota Benga. These attitudes paved the way for the imposition of Western political and economic control over vast expanses of the globe, extending the reach of European power and furthering the incorporation of Africa into the modern age.

The colonization of Africa by European powers during the late nineteenth century was a critical turning point in the history of the African continent, and the world. Between the mid-1880s and the early 1900s Europeans brought nearly 10 million square miles of African territory under their control. Many factors essential to understanding modern world history contributed to this period, known as the "Scramble for Africa": competition for access to natural resources as a result of the Industrial Revolution, the intensification of rivalries between European powers during the age of nationalism, the rise of racist ideologies, and the sense of a civilizing mission that justified the expansion of European empires.

The history of the Congo Free State represents an especially potent subject for studying the particular role of Africa and imperialism in the development of the modern world. The Congo Free State was established in 1885, placing a territory three times the size of Texas under the personal sovereignty of King Leopold. The king validated his claim to the territory at the Berlin Conference, and focusing on his maneuvering to secure the colony opens up exploration of the larger context of imperialism and the "Scramble for Africa." Leopold bolstered his case by appealing to the humanitarian and paternalistic ideals that motivated European imperialism, stressing a commitment to ending the slave trade, and promising to improve the religious and material condition of his African subjects. Despite the humanitarian principles championed by the king, the Congo Free State functioned primarily to exploit the people and the environment of the Congo for the purpose of extracting raw materials like ivory and rubber for profit. These profits rested upon a brutal state-sponsored system of forced labor that resulted in the deaths of millions and an international controversy. This history presents an opportunity to examine the key contradictions of European imperialism, a system that frequently disguised violence and exploitation behind the language of humanitarianism and improvement, and that often used coercion and control to boost the economic interests of nation states and corporations that championed free markets and free trade. The history of the Congo Free State brings imperialism into sharp focus. The levels of violence and exploitation in the Congo Free State were different in degree but not in their essential character from those found in other European colonies.

The use of historical documents in textbooks for introductory history courses has become increasingly popular, but books of this type on Africa are relatively rare. This book seeks to fill that gap. The Introduction examines in five parts the historical significance and the legacy of the Congo Free State. Part 1, "The New Imperialism and the Partition of Africa," describes the key developments and factors that contributed to the rapid expansion of European imperialism during the second half of the nineteenth century. Part 2, "King Leopold and the Congo Free State," examines the particular events and circumstances that led to the creation of the Congo Free State under the rule of the Belgian monarch. Part 3, "In the Rubber Coils," examines the system of colonial rule in the Congo and the impact of the turn-of-the-century rubber boom. The history of Congo rubber is a potent example of how the exploitation of natural resources brought Africans into the global economy of late nineteenth-century industrialization with particularly catastrophic results. Part 4, "The Congo Reform Movement," describes the international campaign that rose up to protest the abuse and exploitation of Africans in the colony, and that eventually forced the king to give up control over the territory. Finally, Part 5, "Legacies of the Congo Free State," examines the legacy of King Leopold's Congo through a concise history of the Belgian colonial and post-colonial eras, highlighting continuing patterns of economic exploitation and the authoritarian control first implemented under Leopold's rule.

Another essential element of all historical inquiry is the analysis and interpretation of primary sources. This book includes a substantial collection of primary sources that complement the general history of the Congo Free State and enable a deeper, more rewarding examination of the issues. The primary source section includes documents and images related to the wider history of imperialism and the "Scramble for Africa," the development of government and trade policy in the Congo Free State, and the international controversy over the abuses committed during the Congo Free State period and beyond. All of these sources also connect to important themes related to world history, such as racism, global industrialization, and nationalism.

The legacies of European imperialism and of Leopold's colonial regime in the Congo have continued to reverberate throughout Central Africa and around the globe in the intervening century. This history brings forward important issues related to the consequences of industrialization and globalization that are especially relevant today. Significant parts of the Congo remain among the poorest, most politically unstable, and most violent regions in the world. This, despite—or perhaps because of—the fact that the Congo is home to several of the most important and valuable natural resources essential to the functioning of modern society. The rise of the modern economy during the age of imperialism set a pattern of African economic development heavily based on the extraction and exploitation of natural resources. This pattern has repeated itself throughout the remaining colonial and post-colonial history of the Congo up to this day. The humanitarian and human rights activism involved in the Congo reform movement also presents an opportunity to examine and discuss issues related to human rights in the twentieth century. Clearly, the history of the Congo Free State is important to understanding many aspects of the modern age of globalization. This book is intended to engage students and instructors with this history and its consequences through an accessible survey of the events and a collection of primary sources that illuminate their global significance

The Congo in 1900

INTRODUCTION

The New Imperialism and the Partition of Africa

The first encounter between the peoples of the Congo and Europe took place in 1482 when the Portuguese explorer Diogo Cão led an expedition down the Atlantic coast of Africa. Near the mouth of the Congo River they found a well-established kingdom with a royal court and center of political authority located in what is now northern Angola. Diogo Cão made two voyages to the region and initiated Portuguese efforts to establish their influence in Africa. In 1487 the ruler of the Kongo people, Manikongo Mzinga Kuwu, embraced a policy of Westernization, welcoming traders and missionaries from Portugal. His son and successor continued the policy, also converting to Christianity and taking the name King Afonso I.

Although the Westernization policy brought some initial technological and commercial benefits, over the forty years of Afonso I's reign the kingdom came under increasing pressure from Portuguese economic interests. During the first decades of the sixteenth century, Portugal took possession of the island of São Tomé and established sugar plantations that required intensive slave labor. Driven by the interests of the planters in São Tomé and other colonies, Portuguese activity in the Kongo shifted from commerce and Christianization to the slave trade. By the 1520s King Afonso was writing impassioned letters to the Portuguese monarch condemning the negative impact of the slave trade on his people. Over the next three centuries the slave trade continued to plague the coastal regions of the Congo, while most of the vast interior of the region remained largely isolated from European interference.

Significant European presence in the Congo renewed during the rapid expansion of imperialist activity in the last decades of the nineteenth century. Between 1870 and 1910 European colonial powers extended their rule over nearly one-fifth of the world's landmass and over one-tenth of its population. In few regions did this change have more impact

1

than sub-Saharan Africa. The industrial modernization of Europe gave the colonial powers the tools, such as rifles and steamships, that enabled them to conquer the continent. Within the span of a few short years Britain, France, Germany, and Portugal claimed almost 80 percent of Africa's territory between them. This so-called "Scramble for Africa" brought dramatic changes to the relationship between Europe and Africa, to the position of Africa within the global economy, and to the lives of millions of Africans who suddenly found themselves under the political authority of a colonial administration.

Historians label this period of dramatic and rapid imperialist expansion the era of "New Imperialism." Late nineteenth-century imperialism was new in several ways, distinct and different from earlier periods of European colonial rule. First, in earlier empires Europeans frequently sent thousands of colonists to live in distant territories. During the New Imperialism there was little of this settler-based colonization. Western powers sent soldiers, explorers, missionaries, and administrators to develop their new colonies, but very few settler families. The numbers of Europeans involved in establishing most African colonies were relatively small, not more than several thousand agents of empire in all. Second, there was a more intentionally imperialist aspect to the era, as compared to the informal imperialism of free trade that characterized the earlier nineteenth century. During the first seventy-five years of the century, Britain's ability to produce cheaper manufactured goods and maintain its naval superiority had led it to champion this informal imperialism where no nation was to interfere with another nation's right to trade. In this system, Britain's commercial might meant that it could almost always come out on top. That naval and commercial power allowed it to exercise enormous informal influence around the globe. In the last decades of the nineteenth century, however, as Germany, the United States, and even Japan arose as economic rivals, pressures emerged to shift course and secure new markets or new resources in formal colonies. As the balance of trade and manufacturing became more equal, the informal imperialism of the midcentury gave way to formal empire and greater protectionism. Especially in Africa, a wave of new colonies, protectorates, and spheres of influence spread across the continent. Finally, while early-modern empires developed over centuries of colonial rule, the New Imperialism took place over a fairly short span of time. In Africa, most of the colonies acquired during the Scramble of the 1880s remained under colonial rule for only seventy-five to eighty years. The era of colonialism in sub-Saharan Africa was relatively brief. However, as we shall see, its consequences were dramatic, and frequently catastrophic.

During the era of New Imperialism itself, observers of the phenomena explained the motives and causes behind it primarily in economic terms. In 1906 the radical British journalist J. A. Hobson argued that overproduction in European economies had led manufacturers and financiers to pressure governments to establish colonies to create new markets for their excess goods and capital. The New Imperialism arose, Hobson argued, as a response to the interests of capitalist manufacturing and banking elites. Similarly, Vladimir Lenin identified imperialism as a symptom of late-stage capitalism, as powerful economic interests pursued profits in colonial ventures. For both Hobson and Lenin, modern industrial capitalism inherently created conditions that led governments to enact imperialist policies.

These authors based their conclusions, in part, on their observation of industrialized Europe's nearly insatiable demand for colonial cash crops and raw materials including sugar, tea, coffee, rubber, palm oil, and cotton during the second half of the nineteenth century. Established powers like Britain, or rising powers like Germany, all pursued colonies to exploit natural resources and to prevent their falling into the hands of rivals. Manufacturers also lobbied to make colonies captive markets for their industrial output, frequently undercutting local production as cheap British textiles did to the traditional handloom weavers of India. To try to maximize the profitability of new colonies, the colonial powers also often resorted to various forms of coerced labor to produce cash crops for global markets. Dutch colonial administrators in the East Indies (Indonesia) forced peasants to plant one-fifth of their land in cash crops like coffee that were resold by the state for significant profit. German and Portuguese colonial governments required cotton production in their East African territories, brutally suppressing opposition by indigenous peoples with force. French and British administrations also used forced labor to build colonial infrastructure through labor taxes. In French West Africa, the colonial state required that "natives" provide up to twelve days of labor per year for projects like railroad construction. In the British Gold Coast, mining companies relied on workers recruited by the state, frequently through quota systems that required village chiefs to provide laborers. King Leopold's Congo became notorious for its brutal regime of coerced labor, but the practice was hardly unique to the Congo Free State in colonial Africa.

Subsequent historical research has shown, however, that Hobson and Lenin's conclusions about the primacy of economic factors in imperial expansion do not entirely hold. While late nineteenth-century capitalists certainly looked overseas for investment opportunities, a larger proportion of their investments went to developed economies like the United States or settler colonies like Canada and Australia. Only a relatively small percentage of foreign investment went to newly established colonies. Newly colonized peoples were often too poor to buy large amounts of manufactured goods, and the cost of developing colonies frequently outstripped the profits from trade. However, at the time economic factors were widely discussed as key elements of imperialism, and imperialists clearly anticipated that they could reap quick profits from the exploitation of raw materials and the acquisition of new markets. King Leopold, as we will see, made enormous profits from the exploitation of rubber in the Congo, but many other colonies were not so profitable. Economics played a crucial role in the era of New Imperialism, but other factors connected to its rise must also be considered.

European political leaders of the late nineteenth century came to see colonies as essential symbols of national power and prestige. Young nations like Germany, Italy, and Leopold's Belgium sought colonies to cement their claims to great power status or to improve their standing on the international stage. Still suffering from its defeat in the Franco-Prussian War, France looked to restore its prestige through expansion of its empire. Britain, the world's established superpower, also felt compelled to defend its own strategic interests through establishing formal colonies. Domestic social and political divisions that resulted from the consequences of industrialization also intersected with imperialist policies. Imperialists argued that colonial success could dampen social class tensions through a wave of celebratory imperial glory. Conservative political leaders frequently used colonial policy and imperialist rhetoric to promote national pride and divert attention away from domestic social tensions. Imperialist propaganda targeted its promises of the economic benefits of empire to working-class and middle-class Europeans alike.

Ideological and cultural factors also contributed to the rise of the New Imperialism. Religious fervor stirred the missionary and humanitarian movements. The intellectual currents of the age also produced racist pseudoscience and social Darwinist ideologies that promoted imperialism. Christian missionaries formed one vanguard of imperialist expansion, and the relationships between missions and colonial governments were complex. Some colonial administrations supported missions if they believed that religious expansion might further their interests. King Leopold encouraged and supported missionary work in the Congo to bolster his humanitarian reputation. At the same time, missionary activism on behalf of colonized peoples and slaves frequently put them at odds with settler and colonial interests. Some of the most vocal critics of Leopold's regime in the Congo were missionaries. Whatever the nature of their relationship to colonial government, missionaries actively encouraged the spread of Western attitudes and practices. By the end of the nineteenth century missionary work emphasized not just proselytizing, but providing medical care, education, and even industrial training to colonized peoples.

Missionaries and imperialists alike justified their actions in the name of this so-called civilizing mission. Humanitarian movements took a moral stand against the slave trade, and practices like polygamy or cannibalism that played into crude stereotypes about African backwardness. Humanitarianism thus contained elements of broader racist attitudes found throughout the imperialist era. Most Europeans shared a view of colonial peoples as heathens and savages, and believed that Europe had an obligation to help uncivilized peoples. During the last decades of the nineteenth century, the rise of social Darwinism and pseudoscientific racism only served to intensify these attitudes. Imperialists concluded that European civilization had clearly come out on top of the struggle for survival, thus justifying imperial conquest.

Technological and medical developments significantly facilitated the conquest of new regions, especially Central Africa. By the 1850s, the use of quinine to treat and prevent malaria had become common practice, dramatically reducing the threat to Europeans posed by the disease in tropical climates. During the eighteenth century, as many as eight in ten Europeans sent to tropical Africa were felled by the disease. Mass production of quinine was common by the second half of the nineteenth century, and the drug was an essential part of any European's travel kit. Quinine did not completely eliminate the threat of malaria, but it reduced it substantially enough that exploration, trade, and conquest in Central Africa became a realistic prospect. More significantly, industrialization gave Europeans an unprecedented technological and military advantage over indigenous populations. Repeating rifles and Maxim guns played a crucial role in putting down anti-colonial resistance and enforcing European hegemony over the continent. Europeans routinely sold older weapons to Africans, but placed restrictions on the sale of these newer models that transformed the balance of military power in the colonial world. Episodes of violent resistance to colonialism erupted in both Africa and Asia, but European military superiority prevailed in all but a few circumstances.

Steam power also changed the scale of the global economy, allowing cargo-hauling steamships to move goods across oceans to and from distant colonies in Africa and Asia. Smaller steamboats made it possible to travel up and down the great rivers of Africa like the Congo, transporting soldiers to enforce colonial rule or manufactured goods and raw materials for trade. Steam-powered locomotives hauled freight cars of raw materials on railroads built to connect the interior of colonies to the coast. In certain regions of Africa these commercial developments allowed for some Africans to profit from the new trade in palm oil and other tropical goods. African farmers in the British Gold Coast planted large numbers of cacao trees to produce cocoa for the global market, dramatically increasing their prosperity in the process. In others areas, like the Congo, the combination of steam power and the booming market for tropical products led to rampant exploitation carried out by the colonial state and its economic partners.

African responses to the New Imperialism varied according to region and circumstances. Efforts at violent anti-colonial resistance were almost always defeated by the superior military technology of the West. Colonial governments also frequently used a strategy of divide and conquer to solidify their power, awarding special privileges to traditional leaders or members of specific ethnic groups to win their allegiance. Local elites recognized that imperial authority gave them opportunities to enhance and maintain their power over their populations. Western-educated professionals and civil servants, including colonial police and soldiers, also assisted the colonial state in exchange for political and economic advantages. Ruling indirectly through native elites and allies allowed colonies to be governed by a smaller number of European agents and officers. Although European powers frequently won and held colonies through military force, their administration also relied heavily on cultural and political means of control.

Throughout the nineteenth century, the industrialization of Europe increased economic activity worldwide and transformed economic relationships around the globe. The resulting boom in international trade and global productivity provided opportunities to increase the wealth of non-European peoples, but the technological and military superiority of the West ultimately forced most colonies to serve the economic interests of their imperial masters. The vast majority of the expanding wealth of the modern age flowed from the colonies to the West. In few parts of Africa was this dynamic more clearly evident than in King Leopold of Belgium's Congo Free State.

King Leopold and the Congo Free State

King Leopold II ascended to the Belgian throne in 1865 at the age of thirty. He was the second king of a small, new nation created in the aftermath of the Revolutions of 1830. The new kingdom had broken away from the Netherlands, and was recognized by the European powers as a neutral, constitutional monarchy. Belgium did go through industrialization before other, larger nations on the European Continent, but its small size and youth meant that it was not a politically or economically significant power. Leopold openly expressed frustration with his status as the constitutional monarch of an inconsequential nation. From the time before he took the throne, Leopold looked overseas to colonies as a way to enhance his power and Belgium's national prestige.

Belgium had few real pre-colonial economic or political connections with sub-Saharan Africa, but Leopold recognized that the looming scramble for control over the trading networks of the African interior might offer him the best opportunity to achieve his imperialist dreams. The Congo River basin was a vast territory in the interior of Central Africa that had remained largely isolated from the impact of the global economy until the second half of the nineteenth century. By the time of King Leopold's reign, this isolation had begun to change. Rising prices for slaves and ivory led Swahili traders from Zanzibar on Africa's east coast to push their caravans further into the regions of the upper Congo and Lualaba Rivers to acquire these valuable commodities. Steamboats facilitated European exploration and navigation of African rivers, as evidenced by Henry Morton Stanley's crossing of the continent by way of the Congo River between 1874 and 1877. Stanley became an international celebrity as a result of his epic voyage, and caught the attention of the ambitious King Leopold.

Leopold had already begun to lay the groundwork for his claim to the Congo through sponsoring geographic conferences and international organizations to support exploration of the region. In 1879 the king hired Stanley to return to the river as an agent of the International Association of the Congo (IAC) to construct a road to bypass the rapids that blocked steamboat access up the river, to establish trading outposts, and most significantly to acquire treaties with African chiefs acknowledging the association's sovereignty over their territories. Stanley returned to Europe with these treaties in hand, and the king was poised to make his move. Emphasizing humanitarian initiatives like ending the East African slave trade, and promising to enact free trade along the river, Leopold began to lobby for international recognition. He first enlisted the support of the United States, and then turned his attention to gaining recognition from European powers at the Berlin Conference.

The impetus for the Berlin Conference of 1884–85 came from the fear that imperialist rivalries in Africa might upset the balance of power in Europe. The French seizure of Tunis in 1881, followed by the British occupation of Egypt the next year, heightened the tensions between European powers and sparked the race to claim colonies in Africa. While Leopold worked to establish his claims to the upper Congo, Pierre Savorgnan de Brazza attempted to assert French control over the northern bank of the river near the Atlantic coast. Germany had sought to validate its great power status through colonial exploration of regions like Togo, Cameroon, and southwest Africa (Namibia). German chancellor Otto von Bismarck called for the participants at the conference to negotiate a new collective policy toward establishing colonies in Africa. Thirteen European nations and the United States attended the conference, but there were no representatives from Africa present. The primary goal of the conference was to extend a measure of international law over the partition of Africa, to bring some order to a process that was already well under way. The attendees established the principle of effective occupation, which stated that nations could validate their claims over colonial territories only if they had treaties with local rulers and established an administration and police force to maintain order. Some historians argue that the significance of the conference has been overstated, but it clearly played an important role in initiating the process of establishing formal imperialism in Africa.

For Leopold the conference presented his best chance to validate his claim to the Congo through recognition of the International Association of the Congo by the major powers. He presented the treaties that Stanley had acquired along the river, he committed the IAC to the goal of ending the East African slave trade, and he pledged that the Congo would be open to free trade. The king had also carefully cultivated his reputation as a humanitarian and philanthropist to strengthen his cause. He engaged in some clever diplomacy, winning the support of France by secretly offering it right of first refusal to purchase the Congo if his venture failed, and convincing the Germans and British that they were better off handing over control of the colony to him than to one of their rivals. These efforts enabled Leopold to win recognition of the IAC's sovereignty over the territory. The IAC, however, had always served primarily as a front for the king's personal interests. On May 19, 1885, the king discarded the IAC and declared the creation of the new Congo Free State. With a territory of nearly 1 million square miles and a population of nearly 30 million people, Leopold at last had his colony.

The colony was unique because it was the property of the king himself. The Belgian government had little interest in an empire, so the king had instead used his philanthropic organizations to acquire a personal colony. Legally speaking, the king acted as a private individual, a kind of colonial entrepreneur. The Belgian parliament did pass a resolution recognizing him as king-sovereign of the Congo Free State, but officially it had no power or influence over the administration of the colony. In the Congo, Leopold could exercise royal power in a way that the constraints of constitutional monarchy in Belgium would never allow. At least that was the vision of the king from his palace in Brussels nearly 4,000 miles away. In reality, the enormous size of the Congo Free State, and the relatively small number of agents and administrators the king hired to govern it, meant that his effective power over the territory was always unstable. The administration of the state was always small. Even by the early 1900s, across nearly a million square miles of territory, it consisted of only fifty stations and about 1,500 European agents. In 1886 the state established the *Force Publique*, a military force made up of European officers and African soldiers. Most of the early recruits came from other parts of Africa, but over the years more and more of the rank and file were forced into service from the peoples of the Congo. Eventually numbering several thousand, the *Force Publique* put down rebellions led by chiefs like Mulume Niama of the Sanga people and Nzansu of Kasai, but was also plagued by regular mutinies of the African troops against their white commanders.

The territory of Leopold's colony was vast, stretching nearly a thousand miles from the Atlantic coast into the interior of Central Africa.

In the east, large portions of the territory still fell under the sway of the slave traders Tippu Tip and Misiri. During the early years, with much of the effort and expense of the colony focused on starting up construction of the Matadi–Leopoldville Railway in the west, the king left power in the eastern half of the colony largely in the hands of the slave traders. Leopold even formally enlisted Tippu Tip, the most powerful of them, to act as governor of the eastern province in 1887. That arrangement, at least temporarily, served the interests of both men. Tippu Tip had an established relationship with Stanley, who played a role in brokering the deal. The slave trader realized that European encroachment threatened to weaken his position, and that of his protector, the Sultan of Zanzibar. Serving the Congo Free State, he hoped, would help to shore up his power and control over the ivory trade in his territory. Leopold gained the advantage of redirecting some of that ivory trade away from Zanzibar, and instead through his own territory down the Congo River. This enabled him to profit from it by putting the trade in the hands of Congo Free State merchants, and subjecting it to Free State customs duties. It also saved Leopold from having to launch a costly war to dislodge Tippu Tip from power. Tensions steadily rose throughout the region, however. Tippu Tip's rivals among his fellow traders and Zanzibari merchants resented his alliance with the Europeans, while his relations with the colonial administration were frequently strained. After the powerful slave trader retired to Zanzibar in 1891, Belgian officers in the region launched an attack on his strongholds. Tippu Tip's son, among others, were defeated after a brutal and violent eighteen-months-long campaign. Agents of the Free State also moved further south to dislodge Misiri from power in the region of Katanga, an area rich with mineral wealth, especially copper. Thus, by 1892 the Congo Free State and the *Force Publique* had established a European presence throughout the eastern territories of the colony.

Efforts to Christianize the Congo followed quickly after Stanley's initial exploration. Protestant missionaries first arrived in the region during the late 1870s. Over the next decade or so, missionaries from Britain, Sweden, and even the United States were active in the territory. Leopold welcomed, and even encouraged, the missionaries to gain their support. During the campaign to secure the Congo, the king pointed to the existence of the missions as proof of his philanthropic intentions. The Berlin agreement stipulated the protection of religious freedom in the Congo; this secured the presence of the Protestant missionaries there even under the rule of the Catholic monarch. By the late 1880s, however, Leopold began to advocate for a Catholic missionary presence as a counterweight to the Protestants. He appealed to the missionary fathers of the Congregation of the Immaculate Heart of Mary, a Catholic missionary society based in Scheut, Belgium, to establish missions in the Free State. The Scheut fathers, who had worked primarily in China up to that point, founded their first posts in the Congo in 1888. The king believed the presence of Belgian missionaries would strengthen the Congo state, and would stimulate interest in the colony among the Belgian people.

Leopold constantly publicized the humanitarian motivations of his work, but he also intended to profit and see a positive return on his investment in the Congo. Here again he turned to Stanley to initiate the enterprise. During the early years the river trade centered primarily on the acquisition of ivory, which was in high demand in late nineteenth-century Europe for making everything from piano keys and jewelry to false teeth. The most important and ambitious project was construction of the railway that would bypass the rapids between the port of Matadi and Leopoldville (present-day Kinshasa). This essential transportation link was required to open up the river to large-scale trade, and connect the raw materials of the interior to oceangoing vessels. Construction on the railroad began in earnest around 1890, requiring a workforce of up to 60,000, not only Congolese but laborers drawn from as far away as the Caribbean and Hong Kong. Thousands died over the course of the eight years of construction on the 240-mile-long railroad.

Controlling and building the colony proved expensive, and began to strain the king's finances. Trade in ivory was profitable, but not sufficient to cover expenses. Leopold had promised to protect free trade in the Congo, but by the late 1880s began to enact policies to regulate and tax trade to his advantage. New regulations meant Africans could sell goods only to the state, and imposed additional restrictions and taxes on trading companies. More significantly Leopold reversed his pledge to not rely on public revenue to fund the Congo Free State. In 1890 he took a loan of 25 million francs from the Belgian state, followed by a second loan of 7 million francs in 1895. During the first decade of his colonial enterprise, Leopold found his financial prospects decidedly precarious.

In the Rubber Coils

Far from the Congo, in 1888, the invention of a Scottish-born veterinarian living near Belfast, Northern Ireland, would set in motion events that dramatically changed King Leopold's fortune. John Boyd Dunlop's invention, the inflatable rubber tire, became a huge commercial success. Cycling enthusiasts and the newly emerging automobile industry pushed up the demand for rubber tires. Rubber also insulated the expanding network of telegraph and telephone wires transforming global communication. The rubber boom of the final decade of the nineteenth century changed the economic prospects of the Congo Free State virtually overnight. Large regions of the Congo were thick with natural rubber vines; so instead of facing potential bankruptcy, the king suddenly found himself in possession of one of the most valuable colonies in Africa.

Leopold had decreed that all land not cultivated or actively occupied by the peoples of the Congo basin was "vacant land" and thereby the property of the state. Since the vast majority of Congolese lived by hunting, gathering, and small-scale cultivation, the result was that almost all of the territory and its natural resources passed directly into the king's hands. He kept a large share of it for himself in what became known as the "Crown Domain," and the rest he portioned out to concession companies, granting them exclusive rights to minerals and raw materials over some 3,000 square miles or more. While these companies were nominally private enterprises, they all had close ties to the king and his agents. In some cases the king and the government reserved the right to a third of the company's profits.

As a result of the international rubber boom, during the 1890s and early 1900s exploitation of these territories focused almost exclusively on the acquisition of rubber. Rubber harvesting became an all-consuming obsession for the king, and the primary path to wealth and promotion for his agents working in the Congo Free State. During the 1890s rubber production in the Free State increased by a factor of twenty, from a few hundred metric tons per year to more than 6,000. Although immensely profitable, obtaining the rubber was difficult and labor intensive. Congo rubber was collected from the wild rubber vines that grew and wound their way up and around tree trunks to the top of the tropical forest canopy. To get at the rubber the collectors had to climb the vines, cut them open with a knife, and collect the sap in a bucket or pot. Collecting sap so high in the canopy was extremely dangerous, and collectors sometimes fell a hundred feet or more to their death. Because the vines were tapped repeatedly they eventually died, forcing collectors to travel farther into the forest to find new vines.

Despite the intense emphasis on cultivating trade, the Congo Free State never developed a currency or other elements of a more advanced economy. Trade and economic activity existed exclusively to exploit the colony's resources for the benefit of the king and his economic partners. Policies in the concession company lands and the Crown Domain imposed a labor tax on the people, who were required to supply food and other necessities to support trading stations and military outposts. Once rubber became in demand, it was quickly incorporated into the system. Government and company agents, many of whose salaries had been cut during the period of fiscal crisis, now worked on commission based upon the amount of rubber collected. Maximizing rubber collections meant agents could as much as double their salaries. Village chiefs were required to supply men who would collect a set quota of rubber on a regular basis, typically every two weeks. Villages that failed to comply were pillaged and burned by the *Force Publique* or armed sentries employed by the concession companies. Individuals who refused to collect rubber, or failed to collect enough, were frequently beaten with the notorious *chicotte*, a whip made from dried hippopotamus hide. For this dangerous work rubber collectors received virtually nothing, sometimes payment in small brass rods traded on the river called *mitakos*, and sometimes knives to be used for cutting more rubber.

The pressure to extract enough rubber to meet international demand, and the incentives for agents to maximize their commissions, led to a steady increase in quotas. The result for many villagers was that collecting rubber became almost a full-time job. In the regions of the colony most affected by the rubber regime, other economic activity ground to a near standstill. Lack of food led to famine and disease. Some villages rebelled, while other villages abandoned their homes and fled into the jungle or to the French Congo in order to escape from the rubber regime. As Africans resisted, the state and the concession companies increased the use of force. Units of the *Force Publique* or company sentries would enter a village to take women and children as hostages. To secure the release of their families men were forced to go into the jungle and return with rubber to meet the regular quota. Most rubber stations contained a *maison des otages* ("house of hostages") where the hostages were kept in overcrowded and disease-ridden conditions. Women were frequently raped, and hostages and rubber collectors could be shot if quotas were not met. Officers in the

Force Publique required their rank-and-file African soldiers to present the hands of victims to prove that they were not wasting bullets, and observers frequently commented on baskets of smoked, severed hands seen at government stations. Some soldiers, if they had missed their targets or gone hunting, would cut the hands off of living villagers to avoid the discipline of their superiors for wasting bullets. Hostage taking had been a common tactic of Swahili traders like Tippu Tip, whose men would take captives from a village and force their relatives to bring back ivory to redeem them. King Leopold had allegedly established the Congo Free State in the spirit of abolishing the slave trade, but in the pursuit of rubber and profit the state adopted the methods of the slave traders as official policy.

The violence of the rubber regime produced a vast fortune for the king. Despite frequent protestations of his commitment to the cause of humanity and progress, little if any of that fortune went to develop the Congo. Instead, Leopold spent lavishly on constructing monuments, parks, palaces, and museums in Belgium. In 1897 he transported nearly 300 Congolese to Europe for an imperialist showcase at Tervuren as part of the Brussels

Nsala, with the severed hand and foot of his five-year-old daughter who was killed as punishment for his failure to meet the rubber quota. The photographer, British missionary Alice Seeley Harris (1870–1970), was a member of the Congo Reform Association. Her photos appeared regularly in publications documenting the atrocities of the Congo rubber regime. (Via Wikimedia; public domain.)

International Exhibition, where more than a million visitors came to see the Africans in model villages. This was the closest King Leopold ever came to his Congolese subjects, for in the more than two decades that he ruled the Congo Free State, Leopold never set foot in his colony. To him, the Congo and its inhabitants were always more a construct or idea, the manifestation of his dreams of empire, power, and profit, an ambitious project that brought violence and destruction to his subjects.

The Congo Reform Movement

For most of the early years of its existence the rest of the world knew little of the Congo Free State beyond the reputation of its ruler. King Leopold kept a fairly tight grip on information about the colony, and what publicity there was served primarily as propaganda to prop up his humanitarian reputation. However, as the implementation of the rubber regime and its violence expanded in the 1890s, rumors about abuses in the territory began to circulate.

Among the first to detail these events was an exceptional African American man by the name of George Washington Williams. A Civil War veteran, he was the first African American elected to serve in the Ohio House of Representatives. During the 1880s he published two influential works of African American history, including the multivolume *History of the Negro Race in America 1619–1880*. Trained as a lawyer and a minister, Williams was also a journalist who published a monthly journal called *The Commoner* in Washington D.C. In 1889 a press syndicate hired him to write a series of articles from Europe, and among them was an interview with King Leopold in Brussels. Williams was intrigued with the Congo Free State. The journalist had long dreamed of a scheme to send enterprising African American men to Africa to assist with education and development projects, and Leopold's Congo Free State seemed like just the place such a venture could succeed.

After his encounter with the king, Williams became anxious to see the colony for himself. He spent nearly six months in the Congo during an 1890 tour of Africa, meeting with government agents, missionaries, and Africans up and down the river. Observing the situation in the colony firsthand Williams came to a shocking conclusion. King Leopold's humanitarian project in the Congo was a fraud. At Stanley Falls, 1,300 miles upriver from the Atlantic, Williams wrote out his observations in an essay that would cause the first international crisis of Leopold's Congo regime. Published in late 1890 as *An Open Letter to His Serene Majesty Leopold II, King of the Belgians and Sovereign of the Independent State of Congo, by Colonel, the Honorable Geo. W. Williams, of the United States of America*, the pamphlet systematically detailed the numerous ways that the administration of the Congo Free State failed to live up to Leopold's lofty humanitarian goals.

Williams' *Open Letter* made a series of dramatic charges. The king and Stanley had largely stolen the Congo from its people through the use of deceptive treaties signed by unwitting chiefs. Despite the king's promises to bring progress and civilization to the peoples of the Congo, the state had done almost nothing to develop schools or hospitals in the colony. Rather than ending the slave trade, the king had relied on forced labor and participated in slave trading by purchasing slaves to use as conscripts in his military force, the *Force Publique*. Williams called upon humanitarian societies and nations throughout the West to investigate the true nature of King Leopold's rule in the Congo Free State. Newspapers published excerpts from the *Open Letter* widely throughout Europe and America, requiring the king and his government to aggressively defend themselves against the charges. His supporters swung into action, they attacked Williams in the press, accusing him of fabricating elements of his personal history and his stories of abuses in the Congo. The Congo Free State government produced a report for the Belgian parliament refuting aspects of Williams' accusations. Williams never got the chance to defend himself—he died of tuberculosis while traveling back to the United States in 1891.

The pamphlet did, however, open the door to wider criticism of the Congo Free State regime. King Leopold had welcomed American and Scandinavian missionaries to the Congo to promote his civilizing project, but during the 1890s they began to write of atrocities committed by agents of the state. These accounts frequently appeared in newspapers and religious magazines across Europe and America. Another who had traveled through the Congo at the same time as Williams was the novelist Joseph Conrad. Appointed by a Belgian trading company to a term as a steamer captain on the Congo River, Conrad spent several months in the colony traveling up the river as far as Stanley Falls. His experiences formed the basis for one of his most famous works of fiction, *Heart of Darkness*. Although not a huge success at the time, the novel's detailed depictions of the horrors of imperialism in the Congo added fuel to the fire of an emerging anti-Leopold campaign.

At about the same time as the publication of *Heart of Darkness*, there emerged from among the critics of Leopold's regime a most effective voice to lead the movement. He was E. D. Morel, a clerk for the Liverpool-based shipping company Elder Dempster. The company moved all of the cargo between Europe and the Congo, and every few weeks Morel traveled to Antwerp to check on the loading and unloading of the cargo ships. Young and inquisitive, Morel raised questions with his superiors about what he saw. Ships arrived from the Congo filled with loads of valuable rubber and ivory, but left carrying no cargo for trade, only chains, explosives, rifles, and ammunition. The company attempted to silence Morel by offering him promotions and more money, but the idealistic clerk refused to stay quiet about what seemed to him clear evidence of slavery or forced labor operating in the Congo. In 1902 he resigned his position at Elder Dempster to take up a career as an activist and journalist, devoting the next several years of his life to exposing the abuses occurring in King Leopold's colony.

Morel began publishing a weekly journal of news from the Congo in 1903. The *West African Mail* included articles criticizing King Leopold's curtailing of free trade in the Free State and accounts of violence and abuses by the *Force Publique*. Morel traveled widely and made speeches, publicizing evidence and information passed on from missionaries and other critics of the regime in the Congo. Morel's articles added to a growing stream of news that led the British Parliament to pass a resolution commissioning a report on the administration of the Congo Free State. The task fell to the British consul located at the Congo Free State capital of Boma, Roger Casement. An Irishman who had worked in the Congo under Stanley during the 1880s, Casement traveled the Congo River for three months in a missionary steamship, interrogating state officials, agents of the concession companies, and Africans. Published in 1904, Casement's report provided detailed evidence of the abuses of the rubber regime, and the use of violence and forced labor that were central to its operation. Morel, with the encouragement of Casement and the missionary Henry Grattan Guinness, established the Congo Reform Association (CRA) to further publicize the plight of the peoples of the Congo. Largely through Morel's tireless efforts the CRA became an international organization, which some have called the first global human rights campaign of the modern age. Morel published several books documenting the atrocities, and drew the attention of world-renowned figures like Mark Twain and Arthur Conan Doyle who contributed their efforts to the cause. Soon the scandal of the Congo became one of the most widely publicized and debated issues of the age. Newspapers and magazines ran weekly updates on the Congo and published photographs of Congolese whose hands had been cut off by soldiers of the *Force Publique*.

King Leopold, as he had done in the wake of George Washington Williams' *Open Letter*, launched a media campaign to refute the accusations of Morel and the Congo Reform Association. He gave interviews to the foreign press, and paid a whole host of agents throughout Europe and America to write books, pamphlets, and editorials praising the accomplishments of the Congo Free State. The growing international pressure on King Leopold, however, forced him to officially address the accusations of violence in the colony. In 1906 he appointed a Commission of Inquiry made up of three judges—one Belgian, one Swiss, and one Italian—to carry out an investigation of the administration of the colony. Leopold anticipated that the commission would provide evidence to absolve him, as investigations in the 1890s had done. This time the results were different. After holding hearings with Africans in the regions of the lower Congo for several months, the commissioners accumulated overwhelming evidence of the abuses committed during the rubber regime. The evidence was so compelling the Belgian government kept the transcripts of testimony classified as a state secret for decades. The summary of the evidence published by the commission was damaging enough to force the king to begin negotiations for transferring control over the colony to the Belgian government.

Legacies of the Congo Free State

In response to the Commission of Inquiry Leopold promised to make administrative reforms, but international pressure and condemnation made this impossible. Negotiations between the king and the Belgian government carried on for more than a year. Leopold had promised in his will to turn the colony over to the state after his death, but would not do so while he was alive without compensation. He also made use of the negotiating period to destroy evidence of abuses in the Congo, and to cover the tracks of his connections to companies operating in the colony. A deal was struck in March 1908; the Belgian government agreed to take on 110 million francs of Congo-related debt, agreed to pay 45 million francs toward building projects (in Belgium not the Congo), and promised the king an additional 50 million francs of future Congo revenues. The Belgian parliament approved the deal in October, and on November 15, 1908, the official transfer of power took place at Boma. The king's health began to fail shortly thereafter, and he died just a year after the loss of his colony in December 1909.

Reformers hoped for big changes to the administration of the colony, the newly renamed Belgian Congo. In particular, they held high hopes for dismantling the system of forced labor, and the new colonial government put an end to the most sensational abuses. It stopped endorsing the cutting off of hands and discouraged hostage taking. However, most of the economic factors that had led to the rubber regime under Leopold remained in some form or another. By 1908 most of the wild rubber vines in the Congo were tapped out. New products and resources, such as cotton or palm oil, emerged to take the place of rubber in the colonial economy, and created new incentives for labor exploitation. Copper, gold, and tin mining all became important concerns in the southern region of Katanga. Hostage taking was no more, but the colonial state imposed a severe head tax that compelled many men to go to work on plantations or in the mines.

The Belgian colonial government also continued the practice of granting concessions to private companies for the right to exploit natural resources in the colony. During the 1910s the British soap manufacturing company Lever Brothers negotiated the rights to purchase almost 2 million acres of land in the Kasai region to harvest palm oil. Lever established the *Huileries du Congo Belge* (HCB) to operate the palm oil plantations, which relied on workers supplied from villages by local chiefs who received payments from HCB in exchange for meeting labor quotas. As production of palm oil increased during the post–World War I period thousands of men, many migrant laborers from far away, were forced to live and work under great hardship on the Lever plantations. In Britain, William Lever was celebrated as a philanthropist who had built a model town at Port Sunlight, near Liverpool, to house his white workers. In the Congo, missionaries and health officers recounted the details of his African workers living in squalor, without adequate medical care, and working under the threat of punishment from the *chicotte*. Concession companies continued to seize control of forest land from local villages, compelled or bribed local chiefs to supply food and laborers, and generally continued many of the policies that were common during the rule of the Congo Free State.

The next major turning point in the history of the Congo was independence, when a former postal clerk, Patrice Lumumba, led a nationalist movement that succeeded in overturning Belgian rule in 1960. Like many former colonies, the newly independent Congo was immediately drawn into the larger dynamics of Cold War geopolitics. Fearing Lumumba's potential ties to the Soviet Union, the United States and Belgium helped to orchestrate his removal from office and eventual execution. The Western powers and commercial interests eventually backed army colonel Joseph-Désiré Mobutu, who consolidated his power over the government by 1965. Mobutu ruled the country for the next three decades through an autocratic, one-party state. He based his political ideology on a doctrine of "authenticity," legitimizing his power through violence and an appeal to allegedly traditional concepts of African leadership. In this spirit, Mobutu changed his name to Mobutu Sese Seko ("all powerful warrior"), and directed the people of Congo to also reject their Christian names. He changed the name of the country to Zaire, based upon a Portuguese adaptation of the Kongo word for the great river, *nzere.*

Supported by Western powers for his anticommunist stance, and by Western corporations who desired access to the country's gold, copper, cobalt, and diamonds, Mobutu became the archetypical strongman. His government became a prime example of a developing world kleptocracy, as he and his associates used their power to divert money to themselves and their business interests. The money stolen by the state was so great that the government of Zaire lacked the resources to perform basic functions. Schools and hospitals went unfunded, and the national GDP declined by more than 60 percent as Mobutu amassed a personal fortune estimated between 4 and 5 billion dollars. This version of one-man rule replicated and eventually drew comparisons to that of King Leopold. The king had been sole proprietor of the Congo Free State, and Mobutu similarly treated the nation's wealth and resources as his own personal possessions. He exploited the land for his own personal gain, and owned a stake in virtually all of the business interests in the country. Like Leopold, Mobutu did not invest these riches in the development of the Congo or its people. Instead he acquired luxury yachts and built grand palaces around the world, including a villa on the French Riviera not far from the site of what had once been King Leopold's own seaside estate.

Mobutu's rule collapsed during the late 1990s in the aftermath of the Rwandan genocide. As the Tutsi-led Rwandan Patriotic Front took over control of Rwanda, millions of Hutu refugees fled into the neighboring eastern Congo, including Hutu soldiers and militia who had committed atrocities in the genocide. Rwandan and Ugandan troops eventually invaded the Congo to assist eastern Congolese rebels against the Hutu militias and the Mobutu regime. In 1998 the new president, Laurent-Désiré Kabila, turned against his Rwandan and Ugandan backers, sparking a second conflict that involved as many as nine different armies and militias fighting for control of land and valuable natural resources in the eastern Congo region. Some 5 million or more people lost their lives in the Congo wars, about as many as are estimated to have died during the era of King Leopold's Congo Free State.

A century after the age of imperialism, the Congo once again finds itself at the center of a technological revolution that shapes its relationship to the global economy. The Congo holds the world's largest deposits of cobalt, a mineral that is a key ingredient in the lithium-ion batteries that power cell phones, laptops, and hybrid cars. Almost two-thirds of the world's cobalt comes from the Congo. More than 100,000 miners toil in mines owned by foreign corporations, or as independent diggers, *crouseurs*, who work hand-dug tunnels to earn two to three dollars a day. Reports from international organizations like Amnesty International detail instances of child labor and the deaths of dozens or even hundreds of miners. Mining corporations have allegedly ignored workplace safety concerns, relocated villages to clear land for mining operations, and underpaid miners, all while collecting enormous profits from cobalt that sells for more than $20,000 a ton on the global market. Now, as a century ago, "the world needs what Congo has."[1] For the peoples of the Congo, it is the cruel irony of their history that the land's wealth in the very resources demanded by the rise of the modern economy has consistently led to suffering and exploitation. The legacies of King Leopold and the "Scramble for Africa" continue to haunt the Congo in the present age of high-tech gadgets and globalization.

---

1. Todd C. Frankel, "The Cobalt Pipeline: Tracing the Path from Deadly Hand-Dug Mines in Congo to Consumers' Phones and Laptops," *Washington Post*, September 30, 2016.

Historiographical Review

For most of the late nineteenth through the early twentieth centuries, the history of Africa, and of imperialism, focused almost exclusively on the motivations and actions of Europeans. As late as the 1960s, the British historian Hugh Trevor-Roper could famously express the view that "at present . . . there is only the history of Europeans in Africa. The rest is darkness."[2] Early works on imperialism, like those of Hobson and Lenin referenced above, tried to account for the different economic, political, and social factors that led to imperialist expansion. In these accounts European economic and political factors typically dominated the narrative; European political and business leaders were the key actors, not Africans or Asians. This perspective characterized almost all works of history on imperialism until the end of World War II.

Challenges to the established narrative of imperialist history during the postwar period emerged on a couple of fronts. Among Western scholars, the British historians Ronald Robinson and John Gallagher pushed the ideas of informal imperialism and the imperialism of free trade to argue in favor of a greater continuity of imperialist policy between the mid-nineteenth and the late nineteenth century. They also challenged the Eurocentric character of earlier interpretations by focusing on events within colonial territories themselves and the motivations of African and Asian collaborators as key factors in the history of imperialism. More significantly, nationalist historians from former colonies also pushed the focus away from Europe and toward Africa. Nationalist histories documented the experiences of colonized peoples, and the rise of anti-colonial movements. A key monument to these developments was the publication of UNESCO's multivolume *General History of Africa*, edited by African historians such as J. F. Ade Ajayi of Nigeria and A. Adu Boahen of Ghana. Strongly influenced by Marxist historiography, some of these works from the 1960s and 1970s remained focused on economic relationships between colonizers and the colonized, but Africanists also consciously sought to reject the notion that Africa was a place without history by telling the story of the previously marginalized peoples of Africa in the pre-colonial and colonial periods.

---

2. Hugh Trevor-Roper, *The Rise of Christian Europe* (London: Thames and Hudson, 1965), p. 9.

Since the 1980s, while historians continued to examine the economic and political causes of imperialism, the cultural turn in colonial and post-colonial studies also introduced a new emphasis on the impact of imperialism on the everyday lived experience of the colonizers and the colonized. Influenced by scholarship from fields like literature and cultural anthropology, these works examined how the colonial encounter changed attitudes about culture, race, gender, and identity in both the colonies and the metropole. Most recently, a new branch of scholarship has sought to further integrate Africa into the emergent field of global history. Historians increasingly identify Africa's central place in the development of modern globalization, as a key link in the slave trade, as a source of essential raw materials, and as the location of some of the most intensive episodes of European imperialism. Knowing Africa's history is thus critical to knowing the history of the world. This book is written in the spirit of that scholarship that aims to interpret both Africa's role in world history, and the impact of global political, economic, and cultural forces in shaping modern Africa.

DOCUMENTS

DOCUMENT 1

Tippu Tip describes meeting the explorer Henry Morton Stanley, 1876.[1]

In the second half of the nineteenth century, Europeans were not the only outsiders to impact the regions of the Upper Congo. The Omani Sultans and Afro-Arab traders based on the island of Zanzibar increasingly sought to expand their influence into the interior of East Africa to acquire ivory and slaves. The best-known and most powerful of these Swahili traders was Hamed bin Muhammed el Murjebi, known to Africans and Europeans by the nickname "Tippu Tip" after the sounds made by the firing of his rifles. Born into an elite merchant family in Zanzibar, he began leading trading caravans into the interior during the 1850s and 1860s. By the end of the 1870s, Tippu Tip had built a trading empire that made him the most powerful figure in East Africa. The influential slave trader also played an instrumental role in the story of King Leopold's establishing control over the Eastern Congo, guiding the explorer Henry Morton Stanley through the region, and serving as a governor of the district during the late 1880s. In this excerpt from his autobiography, Tippu Tip describes his first dealings with Stanley.

I decided on war and we fought the locals for three months until they all announced their submission and willingness to live in peace. All authority

---

1. Source: *Maisha ya Hamed bin Muhammed el Murjebi yaani TIPPU TIP Kwa maneno yake mwenyewe*, historical introduction by Alison Smith, translated by W. H. Whiteley, Supplement to the *East African Swahili Committee Journals* No. 28/2, July 1958 and No. 29/1, January 1959, pp. 109, 111–13.

over them was in our hands, and in the matter of ivory they had no right to sell even the smallest tusk, and any work that we needed doing, they brought men to do it. Food was plentiful, both rice and every other kind. People from Nyangwe came and brought rice in Kasongo, calling the country Bungala because of the quantity of rice. They bought it for ivory. . . .

We stayed for four months, when news came that some Portuguese had come to attack Utetera. I decided to go; on reaching Marera I issued instructions for war and they went and fought with the Portuguese and drove them off. At about this time news came that Said bin Ali Mansur was ill. I decided to return but on the way, news came that he had died. I was deeply grieved. Reaching Nyangwe, I stayed only one day before going on to Kasongo. After the death of Said bin Ali for the next nine months my men were bringing in ivory. . . .

A month passed there until one afternoon Stanley appeared. We greeted him, welcomed him and gave him a house. The following morning we went to see him and he showed us a gun, telling us, "From this gun fifteen bullets come out!" Now we knew of no such gun firing fifteen rounds, neither knew of one nor had seen such. I asked him, "From a single barrel?" He said they came from a single barrel, so I asked him to fire it so we could see. But he said we should produce a fee of 20–30 dollars for firing it once. In my heart I thought he was lying. A single-barreled gun; the second I thought was a cleaning rod! How could the bullets come out of one barrel, one after another? I said to him, "Over in Rumani there is a bow which takes twenty arrows. When you fire, all twenty fly together. And each arrow kills a man." At that he went outside and fired twelve rounds. Then he took a pistol and fired six rounds. He came back and sat down on the verandah. We were amazed. I asked him how he loaded the bullets and he showed me.

Two days passed; on the third he asked me whether I knew Munza. I said, "I neither know Munza nor have I ever heard of the country called Munza." He told me, "If you go to Nyangwe and go north for thirty days you'll get to Munza. Look here, you seem to me like the right sort of person, and I'd like you to take me." I agreed tentatively. "Furthermore," he said, "I'll give you 7,000 dollars." I told him that I wouldn't take him for the sake of 7,000 dollars and showed him the ivory I had, "I shall go from good will and it won't be 7,000 dollars that seduces me from here." Stanley was amazed at the quantity of ivory. . . .

All of my kinsman tried to dissuade me, "You have left your work to follow this European without knowing where he is going?" They gave up trying to dissuade me and I answered them, "I mind my own business not that of other people!" We set off and reached Nyangwe. There the people were more outspoken ... and derided me, "What, going with a European, have you lost your senses? You're mad, will you then become a European? Yet you're not needy, why then? You have your stock of ivory, why then follow an unbeliever?" I told them, "Maybe I am mad, and you that are sensible, keep to your own affairs."

We left Nyangwe, and went north through the forest where one cannot see the sun for the size of the trees, except in the clearings for cultivation or villages. We were in difficulties because of the mud.... This was a blow for the men carrying Stanley's loads and the boat. One day's journey took three days. Stanley was in despair, and he said to me, "What do you suggest? This trouble is serious, what do you say? How many days to the Congo?" I said to him, "We've never been, but it is not far; in six or seven days we should arrive. It is the forest that is the difficulty, but the river is near." He urged us to press on to the river.

We went on until we reached the river Kasuku at the point of its confluence with the Congo from the south (i.e., from the side of its source). By this time we had obtained sufficient boats for Stanley and his loads. We stayed on the Kasuku for twelve days, when Stanley said to me, "Now you return, you have already done me a great service, these last four months or so; let us, however, make one effort to get two large dugouts, sufficient to take my donkey." This was where Stanley and I parted; we stayed up all night on the island to lie in wait for the locals until we got two dug-outs large enough.

Stanley called his men together and told them, "Now Hamed bin Muhammed will return; and you, get busy, for we shall set off on the day after tomorrow. His men replied, "If Hamed bin Muhammed returns we return too; we're not going to a foreign place. Anyway, we signed on at the coast for two and a half years. If Hamed returns we insist on returning too." They were firm in their resolve, the men, not to proceed further. Stanley was very depressed, was even put off of his food, when he went to eat.

During the evening he came to see me and said, "My scheme has foundered if they return, and I shall have to return too. All my trouble will have been for nothing! Will you help me?" I replied, "By the Grace of God I will help you." I slept, and in the morning went to him; I asked him, "Well, what have you decided?" He said, "I have no plans nor do I know what to do." Then I told him, "All right, take my advice and summon all of your men together and speak to me fiercely, say—Look here, if you return, all of my men will insist on returning. Well, my business is the business of the Government, and we are in agreement with Seyyid Bargash. If my men return, then when I return I shall tell Seyyid Bargash that it was Hamed bin Muhammed who ruined my trip; then your property will be seized—when you've said that, well, leave things to me." I left and about noon he called me, collected his men, spoke to me as I had instructed him—before the men—in a harsh tone. I said to them, "Do you hear what Stanley has to say; now set off on the trip and go your way. He who follows me I will kill, because you'll ruin me; my goods will become the property of the Government; on this occasion you have killed me and all my trouble of the past few years is lost. There is no need to die here, is there? But if you follow me I will certainly kill you." I left and they also.

But during the night some of Stanley's headmen came and said to me, "As for us and the European, our time together is finished; we are determined to go back." I said to them, "This won't do, get on with the trip!" They said, "Do you want us to get lost?" I told them that his fate was their fate also; if they got lost they would get lost together. They persisted, "This European is mean; he counts everything out; he doesn't even give us clothes, not one 'shuka' does he offer." I told them to leave this to me, that I would give them what they wanted, only they must get on with the journey. They said, "What shall we do? You we fear and respect for your words, but we've no contract with this European. Our time is almost six months overdue." I told them that their words weren't good enough and that they should follow me. I went to Stanley and told him, "Give me six loads of goods!" He gave me nine. I called the men and told them to take the clothes. To the senior I gave six pieces and to the junior four. To the senior headmen I gave nine pieces to each man, which meant that a little was left over; this I returned to Stanley. They agreed readily to set off. I told Stanley to get moving. He was overjoyed, and in his lying manner, told me, "I don't know how to pay you back, to recompense you for your kindness, nor how much to give you. But when I get back to Europe I shall receive esteem and much wealth. I'll bring you back a watch worth 1,000 dollars, mounted with diamonds, and for money I'll bring you a countless sum, but don't leave here, wait for me a month, until I have passed safely. If I don't find the road I'll come back and we'll go to Rumani."

DOCUMENT 2

Disasi Makulo describes his childhood encounters with Tippu Tip and Henry Morton Stanley, 1883.[2]

The life story of Disasi Makulo vividly illustrates the dramatic changes brought by the development of the nineteenth-century global economy to the peoples of the upper Congo. Traders from Zanzibar advanced from the east to acquire ivory and slaves to work the clove plantations on the island of Pemba, while Europeans arrived from the west to acquire ivory and rubber. The peoples of the Congo found themselves caught between the rival interests of these outsiders. Disasi Makulo was born in a small village on the upper Congo, was captured by Tippu Tip's slave traders, purchased from them by Henry Morton Stanley, educated at a European mission station, converted to Christianity, and eventually returned to his home region as a missionary in adulthood. His autobiography represents a rare example of the African perspective on the period, told in his own voice. In this excerpt from the work, Disasi Makulo recounts his first encounters with Tippu Tip and Henry Morton Stanley.

It was a very hot day. Arriving at a stream called Lohulu, between Makoto and Bandio, my uncle and I decided to take a bath. My Aunt Inangbelema waited for us further along the way. While we were swimming and splashing happily, the *Batambatamba* [slave traders] heard us and surrounded us. My aunt was singing to soothe her crying baby; none of us were aware of the danger.

Suddenly, we heard a cry: "Help! Help! brother Akambu, they are attacking me...."

We jumped quickly from the water, and saw my aunt already in enemy hands. One of the attackers snatched the baby from his mother and tossed it on a red ants' nest. We were so terrified that none of us could get close to him. Uncle Akambu and my cousin fled and hid in the bushes. I stood at a short distance to see what would happen to my aunt. Unfortunately,

2. Source: Makulo Akambo, *La vie de Disasi Makulo: Ancien esclave de Tippo Tip et catéchiste de Grenfell* (Kinshasa: Editions Saint Paul Afrique, 1983), pp. 20–24, 30–32.

one of the men caught sight of me, ran after me, and trapped me. Then my uncle Akambu and my cousin were captured as well.

After our capture, the men took us to the village of Bandio, continuing to capture other people on the way. Later, along the path, some of our men heard the crying baby and found him among the ants. They took him to my parents in Makoto, and these men brought them the news of our capture.

On hearing this, my parents came in haste to find us. Lamenting and weeping, they begged for the men to free us, but the tears and complaints had no influence on them.

After four days, they brought us to the village of Yamokanda. This was the base of their leader, Montipoli or Tippu Tip, and was the place for redeeming captives. Many prisoners were released because their parents brought ivory. My father also brought some ivory tusks, but Tippu Tip told him it was not enough for four people. He freed my uncle Akambu, my aunt Inangbelema, and my little cousin. As for me, he told them, "Go home again and bring back two more ivories." I was left behind with the other prisoners who had not been redeemed.

That same day, after the departure of my parents in search of more ivory, Tippu Tip ordered his soldiers to cross over to Camp Bandu. We left Yamokanda amidst cries, weeping, and wailing. Parents threw themselves on the ground, uttering piercing cries. All of the adults were shackled; as for us kids, we were entrusted to guards ordered to treat us kindly because the Arabs wanted to educate us and make us their fellow citizens.

Soon we reached the river at Bokbili, where several large canoes were loaned to us. One of them was set aside for us, the children. After all of the other captives were loaded onboard, we took our place. Slowly, the canoes drifted into the river. All that you could hear during that dismal journey was the sound of weeping and sobbing. We arrived at last at Bandu. . . .

The next morning, after distributing our meal the keeper presented us with a *mwalimu* [teacher], or Islamic cathechist, who was charged with teaching us to read and write the Quran. Later that day, during our class, another convoy from Yamokanda landed. Among these captives was a man who knew my parents. Speaking to me in our language, he let me know that my father had returned just after our departure with some ivory tusks to redeem me, and he was turned away. Hearing that, I started to cry. . . .

Our master, Tippu Tip, came from time to time to see us, and to make sure we were taken care of properly. He called me DISASI, meaning cartridge; one of my companions, Isalimba, he named MAFUTA, which means oil.

If we children were treated humanely, it was not the same for the adults. They were tortured, wounded, and maimed.

We remained for several months at Bandu, but not in peace. While the Arabs continued to chase the men during the day, the people of Bandu, Bafamba, Basoko and other nearby villages used the night to exact their revenge. Almost every night, they found their way into our camp with spears and sometimes succeeded in killing one or two of the criminals. Because of these frequent attacks by the local natives, the number and power of the Arab soldiers gradually decreased, and food became scarce. Many of the prisoners grew thin, and some even died of starvation.

Tippu Tip, fearing a defeat, saw fit to go up the river to reorganize a new army.

For us, that journey on the river was only a departure to death, although they told us that they wanted to protect us and make us like them. . . .

On the third day we arrived at the village of Ilondo. This place interested our master, and he decided that we would stay there for some time. However, he had to find ways to supply the entire troop. Tippu Tip asked the village chief to regularly supply enough food for the soldiers and the captives. Although this began well, it later became a struggle, because when the food became scarce the soldiers arrested villagers, tortured them and held them hostage until their parents provided everything that Tippu Tip desired.

The *Batambatamba* were not unknown to the inhabitants of Ilondo, although the village was hidden behind a large island. Their wickedness was known throughout the land during the time of their raids. The people who had seen the destruction they had caused among the Lokele, pleaded with the chief and the notables to drive the slave traders from the village. All of the villagers agreed, but they were not good warriors, so they asked for the help of the Topoke. The Topoke, who were good warriors, accepted. Having organized their army they came to Ilondo, bearing spears, with faces painted black and white with coal and chalk. But they had made a mistake, instead of going cautiously they came bellowing loudly, and waving their arms with the hope of an easy victory.

Defeated, the natives returned home to organize for a new battle. Tippu Tip heard this, and ordered his soldiers to join us to leave the place in haste. Before the Topoke had time to attack us again, we set out on route. We crossed the river and this time skirted the right bank.

Eventually a village appeared before us, "Yaomoble, Yaomoble," shouted our guards and the soldiers. When we docked there, the soldiers jumped from the canoes, screaming and shouting at the captives. Our master, Tippu Tip, and some armed soldiers went to the village first to look for lodging. Shortly after, they came back and ordered us all out. . . .

One day, something strange arrived at the village while our *mwalimu* was teaching us to read the Quran. We saw three large canoes coming down the river towards us. Everyone, the villagers and ourselves, were terrified that it was warriors on the way to kill and massacre us. Some villagers fled with their boats to take refuge in the islands, and others ran directly into the forest behind them. As for us, we stayed fixated on the three strange canoes as they docked.

Then we saw white and black men disembark; it was Stanley accompanied by a group of other white men making their journey to found a station in Kisangani (Stanleyville).

Stanley was no longer a stranger among the people of the river. The Lokele called him "Bosongo," which means "albino," a name given to him on his previous voyages on the Congo. No sign of war being evident, Tippu Tip approached the whites. After greeting each other, they began to talk.

Our *mwalimu* took us close to the vessels on the shore. He told us that they were not canoes like ours, but were called boats.

Stanley and his party remained in the village for four days, and then they continued on their journey to Kisangani. . . .

A few days later we saw the three boats on the river again. We saw them arrive, and Tippu Tip went to greet Stanley. After a long conversation between them in an incomprehensible language, Tippu Tip called our guard. He collected us children, and led us over to the two men.

Next we saw workers bring two rolls of cloth and two sacks of salt from the boat. Our *mwalimu* with regret, made it known to us that the white man wanted to buy us.

Stanley started measuring and cutting fabric; for each boy, it was a *doti* (four metres), and for the taller boys, two *doti*. We were twenty-three children, including three girls. At the end, the two men shook hands and one of the workers led us to the boat.

Soon, the three boats moved slowly from the bank, and then accelerated onto the river.

Things were better in our new company, as all those in the boats enjoyed some liberty. We cried, we laughed, we told stories, and no one was ever tied up or treated brutally as in the company of the Arabs.

The day after our departure from Yangonde, we passed through our home region (Yalembu). Astonishingly, the boats did not stop, even though we thought that when we were liberated from the slave traders we would be returned to our parents. I began to cry in our language: "*Ebiso hu ete, ebiso hu ete, toke boitike hu apa!*" (There is our home! There is our home! Let me go to my father!) My companions and I, as on the first day of our capture, took on a new dark sadness. . . .

To calm us, Stanley approached, leaning over the railings to speak to us. We could not understand what he said, so one of his men translated for us in the Lingala language. "My children," he said, "do not be alarmed. I did not buy you in order to injure you, but in order to give you true happiness and prosperity. You have all seen how the Arabs treated your parents and even little children. I can no longer let you return to your home. I do not want you to become like them, wild and cruel people who do not know the True God. Do not regret losing your parents. I will get you other parents who treat you well and teach you good things; then you will become like us."

DOCUMENT 3

Mama Lugeni Dorcas tells of her capture and experiences at a mission station, 1880s.[3]

If African voices from the age of imperialism are relatively uncommon, the voices of African women are even more rare. Mama Lugeni Dorcas met Disasi Makulo at a European mission station, and married him following the early death of his first wife. They had six children, and she assisted him in his missionary work. In this excerpt from La vie de Disasi Makulo, *she describes in her own words her first encounter with Europeans, her capture by warriors from a neighboring village, and her time at the mission station at Bolobo.*

A few days later, my grandmother took me to my mother's house. On arrival, we were told that a man with completely white skin had come to the village, dressed in clothes covering his entire body and without toes. The man, nicknamed "Nkikolesia," had traded jewelry for eggs and chickens.

On the next day, we saw this white man accompanied by a caravan of blacks, among them our chief, Nkoshi. They set off for a nearby village. Along the way they arrived at a stream called Rubi, and the white man asked the chief to carry him across. Our chief refused, telling the white man: "I am the chief, I will not be your porter." Hearing this, the white man became angry, and demanded that the chief carry him across. So, the chief told the white man to climb on his back, and carried him to the middle of the stream before dropping him into the water and returning home.

Seeing our chief return, the entire village reacted with joy because we thought that the white man had taken our chief to kill him.

At that time, I did not know anything about the war. But one day, we saw a great coming and going about the village; people moved their belongings hastily beyond the river Rubi. At night there was a heavy rain.

---

3. Source: Makulo Akambo, *La vie de Disasi Makulo: Ancien esclave de Tippo Tip et caté-chiste de Grenfell* (Kinshasa: Editions Saint Paul Afrique, 1983), pp. 64–70.

Towards the dawn, while we were fast asleep, we were awoken by the sound of Basongo warriors who had secretly encircled the village. As people tried to escape our village they fell directly into the hands of the enemy. My mother, who had a baby a few weeks old, and my brothers were captured. One of the attackers took the baby and threw it aside. After being soundly beaten, all of the captives were taken to a central place to be held. I witnessed this cruel scene hidden in the grass, and then followed the crying to where everyone was gathered. These assailants did not want to spare the infants, who like my little brother were massacred without mercy. My grandmother, Banlosi, who came after us was also captured and killed. . . .

After a few days we learned that a white man would fight our enemies to deliver us. Our masters also heard this, and began to sell their captives.

Soon, the whites came, a state agent accompanied by a good number of soldiers. He summoned the chief and told him that he wanted to redeem all of the captives. He brought out a trunk full of various kinds of jewelry, necklaces, *mitakos*, fabrics, etc. Struck by the beauty of these objects, the chief gave us to the European. After having delivered us, the white man took us to Lusambo.

That same day, a small boat called Kiapo, driven by a white man, arrived at Lusambo. The agent told us that it would take us to a Protestant mission in Kintambo. There we met a lot of boys and girls from different tribes who had been redeemed like us. At the mission station we came under the protection of a missionary doctor, Dr. Sims. . . .

On his departure for Europe, Dr. Sims sent us to the care of other whites; two boys, another girl and me were sent to the Missionary George Grenfell, who brought us to Bolobo.

Bolobo was already a developed post, with well-built houses for the Europeans, a camp for the mission personnel, a boarding school for girls, and a chapel. At school we were taught to read, write, and do math. We had sewing, knitting, drawing lessons, and other work. We did religion and singing lessons together with the boys. . . .

Our missionaries treated us children well. They provided us rooms, beautiful clothes and especially taught us many things to help our future. To preserve us from all possible future troubles, the missionaries wished for us to marry other young Christians educated by them. Thus after the death of Sara, they arranged for me to marry Disasi. This was done.

DOCUMENT 4

Treaty between the International Association of the Congo and African chiefs, 1884.[4]

During the 1870s, King Leopold created the International African Association and the International Association of the Congo as front organizations to further his campaign to establish a colony in the Congo region. Between 1879 and 1884, the king sent the celebrated explorer Henry Morton Stanley to the Congo as his appointed agent to establish treaties with native leaders that gave rights to their lands and resources to the IAC. This document is an example of one of these treaties that King Leopold used as the legal basis for his claim to the territories that eventually became the Congo Free State.

Expédition Internationale du Haut-Congo

South Manyanga Station, March 31, 1884

We, the chiefs Dongosi and Kukuru of Voonda, sole masters of the district of that name, having applied to Henry M. Stanley, Chief of the Expédition Internationale du Congo, to enter into that confederacy of native chiefs now established between Stanley Pool and South Manyanga, and all of the responsibilities and privileges undertaken or enjoyed by the members of that confederacy being explained to us, we hereby enter into an agreement with the said Henry M. Stanley, and bind ourselves, our heirs and successors, to observe the following articles:—

I.—We shall keep all roads passing through our district free of duty, tax or impost to all strangers, white or black, who shall have the recommendation or good-will of the Association Internationale Africaine.

II.—We surrender all right to collect taxes or imposts to the agents of the said Association.

4. Source: Henry Morton Stanley, *The Congo and the Founding of Its Free State: A Story of Work and Exploration*, vol. II (New York, 1885), p. 206.

III.—We agree to recognize the sovereignty of the said Association, and adopt the flag of the Association, blue, with a golden star, as a sign thereof.

IV.—We shall refer to the said Association all matters relating to the government, all questions affecting the peace of the country, all troubles between ourselves and neighbours, or between ourselves and strangers of any colour or nationality, to the arbitration and decision of the Agent of the Association Internationale Africaine.

V.—We declare that we have not made any agreement, oral or written, with any person that would render this agreement null and void in any particular.

VI.—We declare that from henceforth we and our successors and subjects shall abide by the decision of the Chief Agent of the Association Internationale Africaine in all matters affecting our welfare, our possessions, or our relations to our neighbours, or strangers of any colour, and that we shall not act contrary to the spirit of this agreement in any particular, on pain of forfeiting all subsidies, gifts, or presents made to us by the agents of the Association. In witness whereof we have set our confidential servants as our proxies to sign this agreement, having understood its contents and given our consent verbally in presence of our people to do and act precisely as the chiefs of Ngombi, Luteté, and Makitu have already done.

Witnesses—
Mdombasi Luboki, his X mark
Dualla.
Proxy for the Chief Dongosi
Lofunsu li Mbulu, his X mark
Proxy for the Chief Kukuru

DOCUMENT 5

President of the United States Chester A. Arthur's State of the Union address, 1883.[5]

In April 1884 the United States became the first nation to formally recognize the International Association of the Congo's claim to the territory that would become the Congo Free State. King Leopold used several agents in America to successfully lobby for the support of President Chester A. Arthur, emphasizing free trade, humanitarianism, and the involvement of the Welsh-American Henry Morton Stanley in the enterprise. Although the United States did not involve itself much directly in the "Scramble for Africa," this excerpt from President Arthur's 1883 State of the Union address shows the American administration's particular interest in the affairs of the Congo.

The rich and populous valley of the Kongo is being opened to commerce by a society called the International African Association, of which the King of the Belgians is the president and a citizen of the United States the chief executive officer. Large tracts of the territory have been ceded to the association by native chiefs, roads have been opened, steamboats placed on the river, and the nuclei of states established at twenty-two stations under one flag which offers freedom to commerce and prohibits the slave trade. The objects of the society are philanthropic. It does not aim at permanent political control, but seeks the neutrality of the valley. The United States can not be indifferent to this work nor to the interests of their citizens involved in it. It may become advisable for us to cooperate with other commercial powers in promoting the rights of trade and residence in the Kongo Valley free from the interference or control of any one nation.

---

5. Source: *State of the Union,* http://stateoftheunion.onetwothree.net/texts/18831204 html.

DOCUMENT 6

General Act of the Berlin Conference, 1885.[6]

The participants at the Berlin Conference of 1884–85 sought to replace the ad hoc system of colonial arrangements and treaties between European powers and individual African chiefs with an international agreement on regulating colonization and trade in sub-Saharan Africa. All of the major Western powers sent representatives, but no Africans were invited to attend. Convened by Chancellor Otto von Bismarck, the conference reflected Germany's desire to claim global power status and to acquire an African empire. It also afforded King Leopold the chance to lobby for and legitimate his claim to the Congo. In these excerpts from the General Act approved by the conference participants, note two key commitments made by Leopold to bolster his case: (1) a guarantee of free trade in the Congo territory, and (2) an effort "to employ all means at [his] disposal" to eliminate the slave trade.

General Act of the Conference of Berlin Concerning the Congo.

Signed at Berlin, February 26, 1885.
In the name of Almighty God:

The President of the United States of America, His Majesty the Emperor of Germany, King of Prussia, His Majesty the Emperor of Austria, King of Bohemia etc., and Apostolic King of Hungary. His Majesty the King of the Belgians, His Majesty the King of Denmark, His Majesty the King of Spain, the President of the French Republic, Her Majesty the Queen of the United Kingdom of Great Britain and Ireland, Empress of India, His Majesty the King of Italy, His Majesty the King of the Netherlands, Grand Duke of Luxembourg, His Majesty the King of Portugal

6. Source: "General Act of the Conference of Berlin Concerning the Congo," Supplement: Official Documents, *American Journal of International Law* 3, no. 1 (1909): pp. 7–25, http://www.jstor.org/stable/2212022.

and Algarves, etc. etc. etc., his Majesty the Emperor of All the Russians, His Majesty the King of Sweden and Norway etc. etc., and His Majesty the Emperor of the Ottomans.

Wishing to regulate in a spirit of good mutual understanding the conditions most favorable to the development of commerce and of civilization in certain regions of Africa, and to assure to all peoples the advantages of free navigation upon the two principal African rivers which empty into the Atlantic ocean; desirous on the other hand to prevent misunderstandings and contentions to which the taking of new possessions on the coast of Africa may in future give rise, and at the same time preoccupied with the means of increasing the moral and material well-being of the indigenous populations, have resolved, upon the invitation which has been addressed to them by the Imperial Government of Germany in accord with the Government of the French Republic, to assemble for this object a Conference at Berlin. . . .

Who, furnished with full powers which have been found in good and due form, have successively discussed and adopted:

1st. A Declaration relative to the liberty of commerce in the basin of the Congo, embouchures and neighboring countries, with certain dispositions connected therewith;

2nd. A Declaration relative to the slave trade, and the operations which on sea or land furnish slaves for the trade;

3rd. A Declaration relative to the neutrality of the territories comprised in the conventional basin of the Congo;

4th. An Act of navigation of the Congo, which, while taking note of local circumstances, extends to this river, to its affluents, and the waters which are assimilated to them, the general principles announced in Articles 108 to 116 of the final Act of the Congress of Vienna and designed to regulate, between the Powers signatory to said Act, the free navigation of navigable water courses which separate or traverse several States, principles since then conventionally applied to certain rivers of Europe and America, and notably to the Danube, with the modifications provided by the Treaties of Paris of 1856, of Berlin of 1878, and of London of 1871 and of 1883;

5th. An Act of navigation of the Niger which, while equally taking note of local circumstances, extends to this river and to its affluents the same principles inscribed in Articles 108 to 116 of the final Act of the Congress of Vienna;

6th. A Declaration introducing into international relations certain uniform rules relative to the occupations which may take place in the future on the coast of the African continent;

And having judged that these different documents might be usefully coordinated in a single instrument, have collected them into a general Act composed of the following articles.

Chapter I
DECLARATION RELATIVE TO THE LIBERTY OF COMMERCE IN THE BASIN OF THE CONGO, ITS EMBOUCHERES AND NEIGHBORING COUNTRY AND DISPOSITIONS CONNECTED THEREWITH

Article 6

Depositions relative to the protection of the natives, of missionaries and of travelers, and also to religious liberty.

All powers exercising rights of sovereignty or an influence in the Said territories engage themselves to watch over the conversion of the indigenous populations and the amelioration of their moral and material conditions of existence and to strive for the suppression of slavery and especially of the negro slave trade; they shall protect and favor without distinction of nationality or of worship, all the institutions and enterprises religious, scientific or charitable, created and organized for these objects or tending to instruct the natives and to make them understand and appreciate the advantages of civilization.

The Christian missionaries, the savants, the explorers, their escorts, properties and collections shall be equally the object of special protection.

Liberty of conscience and religious toleration are expressly guaranteed to the natives as well as to allegiants and to strangers.

The free and public exercise of all forms of worship, the right to erect religious edifices and to organize missions belonging to all forms of worship shall not be subjected to any restriction or hindrance. . . .

Chapter II
DECLARATION CONCERNING THE SLAVE TRADE

Article 9

Conformably to the principles of the law of nations, as they were recognized by the signatory Powers, the slave trade being interdicted, and as the operations which, by land or sea, furnished slaves to the trade ought to be equally considered as interdicted, the Powers who exercise or shall exercise rights of sovereignty or an influence in the territories forming the conventional basin of the Congo declare that these territories shall not serve either for a market or way of transit for the trade in slaves of any race whatever. Each of these Powers engages itself to employ all the means in its power to put an end to this commerce and to punish those who are occupied in it.

DOCUMENT 7

A European missionary condemns
the African slave trade, 1890.[7]

Nineteenth-century humanitarians and missionaries frequently emphasized the benefits derived from the introduction of Christianity, commerce, and civilization to the African continent. In particular, they presented the existence of slavery and slave trading in Africa as a key justification for the expansion of European imperialism on the continent. King Leopold put the abolition of the Afro-Arab slave trade, based in Zanzibar, at the center of his humanitarian project in the Congo. The idea of the civilizing mission also contained key elements of the racist attitudes common to the age of imperialism, viewing colonized peoples as heathens and savages, or characterized by essential racial characteristics. Fanny E. Guinness and her husband, Henry Grattan Guinness, founded a missionary training college in East London, and participated in the creation of the Congo and Balolo Mission (1889). In this excerpt from her book on the founding of the mission, Guinness describes the slave trade as a cancer threatening Africa, and provides a general view of the attitudes common to humanitarian imperialists of the time.

As a malignant and incurable cancer eats with intolerable anguish into the body, until death ensues, so does this evil eat into the vitals of Africa, with results that must be fatal, unless it can be arrested. . . .

We allude of course to the destructive and depopulating ARAB SLAVE-TRADE. . . .

Their contempt of lower races, and their unprincipled greed of gain; the slavery which their customs demand and their faith allows; their partial civilization and possession of firearms, and the helpless, unarmed condition of most of the native races—all these together have made them what they undoubtedly are, Africa's worst woe! Like ravenous beasts,

---

7. Source: Mrs. H. Grattan Guinness, *The New World of Central Africa with a History of the First Christian Mission on the Congo* (London: Hodder & Stoughton, 1890), pp. 116–19.

they live by carnage, and never even accuse themselves of cruelty. They are born and clever traders. Ivory is almost the only article of African commerce which as yet yields much profit. It abounds all over the interior, and can be bought so cheaply there that enormous profits arise from its sale on the coast. But it cannot walk itself, and there are no trains or beasts of burden to carry it. How is it to be got to the seashore? If porters were honestly paid to carry it, the profits would be seriously diminished; and besides, porters would not spontaneously undertake the long, difficult, and dangerous journey.

The easiest, cheapest, and almost only way to get riches by this commerce is to *steal* and enslave men and women, manacle them that they may not escape, load them with the heavy tusks, drive them under the lash, give them only food enough to keep them from starvation, shoot them if they faint and drop, and sell *them* as well as their loads, when the long journey is ended. This is what the Arabs do.

DOCUMENT 8

Letter from King Leopold to the prime minister of Belgium, 1890.[8]

The Congo Free State was not like other colonies because it was not the possession of the Belgian state. Rather, the king ruled the colony as his personal property, as sovereign and proprietor. At the formation of the CFS in 1885, Leopold pledged that he would support the colony from his personal finances, and not rely on the resources of the state. However, by 1890 it was clear that the colony was not profitable, and had become a significant drain on the king's purse. As a result the king was forced to take a substantial loan from the Belgian government to keep the colony afloat. In this letter written to Prime Minister Auguste Beernaert shortly after the loan was approved, Leopold declares his intention to will the colony to the Belgian state after his death, "to make it easy for Belgium to profit from my work."

Dear Minister,

I have never ceased to draw the attention of my compatriots on the need to turn our view towards overseas territories.

History teaches us that countries with small territories have a moral and material interest in extending their influence beyond their narrow borders. Greece founded opulent cities, home to arts and civilization, on the shores of the Mediterranean. Later, Venice built its grandeur on its maritime and commercial relations no less than on its political success. The Netherlands have thirty million subjects in the Indies who trade tropical products for the products of the mother country.

It is in this service to the cause of humanity and progress that subordinated peoples appear as useful members to the great family of nations. More than any other, a trading and manufacturing nation like ours must do its best to secure opportunities for its workers, whether intellectual,

---

8. Source: Constant Leclère, *La formation d'un Empire colonial Belge*, in Jean Deharveng, *Histoire de la Belgique contemporaine*, ed. Albert Dewit, vol. 3, 1830–1914 (Brussels, 1930), p. 599.

capitalist, or manual. These patriotic concerns have dominated my life. They are what caused the creation of the African effort.

My plans were not sterile: a young and vast State, led from Brussels, has peacefully taken its place in the sun, thanks to the kind support of the powers which have applauded its beginning. Belgians administer it, while other compatriots, more and more every day, are already making a profit on their capital.

The vast river system of the Congo opens the way for rapid and economical channels of communication that will allow us to penetrate directly into the center of Africa. The construction of the railroad around the cataract, now assured thanks to the recent vote of the legislature, will significantly increase the ease of access. Under these conditions, a great fortune is reserved for the Congo, whose immense value will soon shine for all to see.

The day after this memorable act, I thought it my duty, when death will come to strike me, to make it easy for Belgium to profit from my work, as well as that of those who helped me to found and direct it and to whom I give thanks here once again. Thus did I make, as sovereign of the Congo Free State, the will that I am sending to you; I will request that you share it with the Legislative Chambers at the time you deem most appropriate.

The beginning of endeavors such as those that have so preoccupied me is difficult and expensive. I insisted upon bearing the costs. A king, in order to give service to his country, must not fear to design and promote the realization of a project so reckless in appearance. The wealth of a sovereign consists of public prosperity. That alone can appear to his eyes as an enviable treasure, which he should try to constantly build up. Until the day I die, I will continue with the same thoughts of national interest that have guided me until now, to direct and sustain our African efforts, but if, without waiting for that day, it makes sense for the country to contract closer ties with my Congo possessions, I would not hesitate to do it, I would be happy, while I am alive, to see it in full benefit towards the Chambers as towards the Government for the aid that they gave to me on several occasions in this creation. I think that I am right in saying that Belgium will gain genuine advantages and will see opening before her, on a new continent, happy and wide perspectives.

Your very devoted,
Leopold

DOCUMENT 9

George Washington Williams criticizes King Leopold's rule in the Congo, 1890.[9]

The African American minister, lawyer, journalist, and activist George Washington Williams is today less well known than many other more famous figures who publicized or commented on the abuses of King Leopold's rule in the Congo. However, his Open Letter to His Serene Majesty Leopold II *was one of the earliest and most important documents to call attention to the plight of the Congolese. After serving in the American Civil War as a teenager, Williams went on to various careers during the 1870s and 1880s. In 1889–90 he traveled to the Congo Free State, lured in part by the stories of the improvement of the condition of the African population put out by Leopold's propaganda machine. His* Open Letter *to the king scathingly criticized Leopold for failing to live up to his promises.*

Good and Great Friend,

I have the honour to submit for your Majesty's consideration some reflections respecting the Independent State of Congo, based upon a careful study and inspection of the country and character of the personal Government you have established upon the African continent.

It afforded me great pleasure to avail myself of the opportunity afforded me last year, of visiting your State in Africa; and how thoroughly I have been disenchanted, disappointed and disheartened, it is now my painful duty to make known to your Majesty in plain but respectful language. Every charge which I am about to bring against your Majesty's personal Government in the Congo has been carefully investigated; a list of competent and veracious witnesses, documents, letters, official records

9. Source: "An Open Letter to His Serene Majesty Leopold II, King of the Belgians and Sovereign of the Independent State of Congo By Colonel, The Honorable Geo. W. Williams, of the United States of America," in A. Cromwell Hill and Martin Kilson, *Apropos of Africa: Sentiments of Negro American Leaders on Africa from the 1850s to the 1950s,* 1st ed. (New York: Routledge, 2014), pp. 98–108.

and data has been faithfully prepared, which will be deposited with Her Britannic Majesty's Secretary of State for Foreign Affairs, until such time as an International Commission can be created with power to send for persons and papers, to administer oaths, and attest the truth or falsity of these charges.

When I arrived in the Congo, I naturally sought for the results of the brilliant programme: "fostering care," "benevolent enterprise," an "honest and practical effort" to increase the knowledge of the natives "and secure their welfare." I had never been able to conceive of Europeans, establishing a government in a tropical country, without building a hospital; and yet from the mouth of the Congo River to its head-waters, here at the seventh cataract, a distance of 1,448 miles, there is not a solitary hospital for Europeans, and only three sheds for sick Africans in the service of the State, not fit to be occupied by a horse. Sick sailors frequently die on board their vessels at Banana Point; and if it were not for the humanity of the Dutch Trading Company at that place—who have often opened their private hospital to the sick of other countries—many more might die. There is not a single chaplain in the employ of your Majesty's Government to console the sick or bury the dead. Your white men sicken and die in their quarters or on the caravan road, and seldom have Christian burial. With few exceptions, the surgeons of your Majesty's Government have been gentlemen of professional ability, devoted to duty, but usually left with few medical stores and no quarters in which to treat their patients. The African soldiers and labourers of your Majesty's Government fare worse than the whites, because they have poorer quarters, quite as bad as those of the natives; and in the sheds, called hospitals, they languish upon a bed of bamboo poles without blankets, pillows or any food different from that served to them when well, rice and fish.

I was anxious to see to what extent the natives had "adopted the fostering care" of your Majesty's "benevolent enterprise," and I was doomed to bitter disappointment. Instead of the natives of the Congo "adopting the fostering care" of your Majesty's Government, they everywhere complain that their land has been taken from them by force; that the Government is cruel and arbitrary, and declare that they neither love nor respect the Government and its flag. Your Majesty's Government has sequestered their land, burned their towns, stolen their property, enslaved their women and children, and committed other crimes too numerous to mention in detail. It is natural that they everywhere shrink from "the fostering care" your Majesty's Government so eagerly proffers them. . . .

EIGHTH.—Your Majesty's Government has violated the General Act of the Conference of Berlin by firing upon native canoes; by confiscating the property of natives; by intimidating native traders, and preventing them from trading with white trading companies; by quartering troops in native villages when there is no war; by causing vessels bound from "Stanley-Pool" to "Stanley-Falls" to break their journey and leave the Congo, ascend the Aruhwimi river to Basoko, to be visited and show their papers; by forbidding a mission steamer to fly its national flag without permission from a local Government; by permitting the natives to carry on the slave-trade, and by engaging in the wholesale and retail slave-trade itself. . . .

TENTH.—Your Majesty's Government is engaged in the slave-trade, wholesale and retail. It buys and sells and steals slaves. Your Majesty's Government gives £3 per head for able-bodied slaves for military service. Officers at the chief stations get the men and receive the money when they are transferred to the State; but there are some middle-men who only get from twenty to twenty-five francs per head. Three hundred and sixteen slaves were sent down the river recently, and others are to follow. These poor natives are sent hundreds of miles away from their villages, to serve among other natives whose language they do not know. When these men run away a reward of 1,000 N'taka is offered. Not long ago such a recaptured slave was given 100 "chikote" each day until he died. Three hundred N'taka—brassrod—is the price the State pays for a slave, when bought from a native. The labour force at the stations of your Majesty's Government in the Upper River is composed of slaves of all ages and both sexes. . . .

TWELFTH—The agents of your Majesty's Government have misrepresented the Congo country and the Congo railway. Mr. H. M. STANLEY, the man who was your chief agent in setting up your authority in this country, has grossly misrepresented the character of the country. Instead of it being fertile and productive it is sterile and unproductive. The natives can scarcely subsist upon the vegetable life produced in some parts of the country. Nor will this condition of affairs change until the natives shall have been taught by the European the dignity, utility and blessing of labour. There is no improvement among the natives, because there is an impassable gulf between them and your Majesty's Government, a gulf which can never be bridged. HENRY M. STANLEY'S name produces a shudder among this simple folk when mentioned; they remember his broken promises, his copious profanity, his hot temper, his heavy blows, his severe and rigorous measures, by which they were mulcted of their lands. His last appearance in the Congo produced a profound sensation among them, when he led 500 Zanzibar soldiers with 300 camp followers on his way to relieve EMIN PASHA. They thought it meant complete subjugation, and they fled in confusion. But the only thing they found in the wake of his march was misery. No white man commanded his rear column, and his troops were allowed to straggle, sicken and die; and their bones were scattered over more than 200 miles of territory.

CONCLUSIONS

Against the deceit, fraud, robberies, arson, murder, slave-raiding, and general policy of cruelty of your Majesty's Government to the natives, stands their record of unexampled patience, long-suffering and forgiving spirit, which put the boasted civilisation and professed religion of your Majesty's Government to the blush. During thirteen years only one white man has lost his life by the hands of the natives, and only two white men have been killed in the Congo. Major Barttelot was shot by a Zanzibar soldier, and the captain of a Belgian trading-boat was the victim of his own rash and unjust treatment of a native chief.

All the crimes perpetrated in the Congo have been done in your name, and you must answer at the bar of Public Sentiment for the misgovernment of a people, whose lives and fortunes were entrusted to you by the August Conference of Berlin, 1884–85. I now appeal to the Powers which committed this infant State to your Majesty's charge, and to the great States which gave it international being; and whose majestic law you have scorned and trampled upon, to call and create an International Commission to investigate the charges herein preferred in the name of Humanity, Commerce, Constitutional Government and Christian Civilisation.

I base this appeal upon the terms of Article 36 of Chapter VII of the General Act of the Conference of Berlin, in which that August assembly of Sovereign States reserved to themselves the right "to introduce into it later and by common accord the modifications or ameliorations, the utility of which may be demonstrated experience."

I appeal to the Belgian people and to their Constitutional Government, so proud of its traditions, replete with the song and story of its champions of human liberty, and so jealous of its present position in the sisterhood of European States—to cleanse itself from the imputation of the crimes with which your Majesty's personal State of Congo is polluted.

I appeal to Anti-Slavery Societies in all parts of Christendom, to Philanthropists, Christians, Statesmen, and to the great mass of people everywhere, to call upon the Governments of Europe, to hasten the close of the tragedy your Majesty's unlimited Monarchy is enacting in the Congo.

I appeal to our Heavenly Father, whose service is perfect love, in witness of the purity of my motives and the integrity of my aims; and to history and mankind I appeal for the demonstration and vindication of the truthfulness of the charge I have herein briefly outlined.

And all this upon the word of honour of a gentleman, I subscribe myself your Majesty's humble and obedient servant.

GEO. W. WILLIAMS
Stanley Falls, Central Africa,
July 18th, 1890.

DOCUMENT 10

The Belgian parliament discusses the Congo, 1891.[10]

George Washington Williams' Open Letter to His Serene Majesty Leopold II sparked the first international controversy surrounding the administration of the Congo Free State. The king organized a vigorous campaign to discredit Williams. In June 1891 members of the Belgian parliament took up the topic in a debate. In this excerpt from the parliamentary record the prime minister, Auguste Beernaert, defends the government of the Congo Free State and promises the members of the assembly that an inquiry will absolve the administration of the charges. By the end of the summer the top administrators of the CFS produced a nearly fifty-page report defending the government and refuting Williams' accusations. Although the Belgian government did not control the Congo Free State, it is clear that members of the assembly felt that its national reputation was on the line.

M. Carlier—A book is currently causing a lot of noise not only in Belgium, but especially in some of the foreign press.

To believe these libels to be true, the Congo State would be the scene of unspeakable acts of savagery, and that these acts are committed with the connivance, almost with the encouragement of the authorities. It shows a kind of abuse or tyranny that one would have to go back to the times of barbaric conquests to find equivalent horrors. Far from destroying the hideous source of slavery, we would be making the wound more vivid and bloody as ever in West Africa. . . .

I have no doubt that there are explanations. . . . I therefore respectfully request the Government would be able to provide, on the occasion of the next extraordinary budget, some information on the results already achieved in the Congo, and how the facts became so strangely disfigured.

M. Beernaert—We have seen more unexpected allegations. This state, founded mainly to ensure the suppression of trafficking; that state, without which Central Africa would be devastated and depopulated all

---

10. Source: *Chambre des Representants—Annales Parlementaires, Séance du 18 Juin 1891*; Public Record Office, National Archives Kew: F.O. 84 2118 ERD/2821.

the way to Leopoldville and perhaps to Boma, it (Williams' document) represents him (the King) as the trafficker!

As the honorable M. Carlier said earlier, it would be excess and horrors every day; immorality built into a system. It would be unheard of if our officers, missionaries, Belgians of all ranks and conditions in the Congo were found to be agents, accomplices, or silent witnesses to this criminal policy!

And the number of these witnesses renders the business difficult. There are in the state today in Africa, 746 whites, over half of them compatriots.

It would assume the complicity of all of these people!

As far as I am concerned, I am not moved at all by charges we have seen repeated at almost every phase of the Congo. Their very enormity is enough to deny them.

But the directors of the Congo—gallant men, you all know—sorely feel the unworthiness of these attacks, and I know they will complete a report to the sovereign that will summarize the considerable, and remarkable, results already obtained in Africa, and doing so, at least implicitly, judge the gossip and false rumors.

This report will, I do not doubt, be communicated to the legislature and no doubt will give satisfaction to the desire expressed by the honorable M. Carlier. The government will also undertake to provide any additional clarifications he might ask of them, and would be happy to contribute to the destruction of this strange legend of absolute secrecy surrounding the administration of these vast territories opened to travel and trade in every way.

DOCUMENT 11

Joseph Conrad's *Heart of Darkness*, 1899.[11]

Conrad's short novel is probably the most famous, and most widely read, of all works of fiction on the topic of European imperialism in English literature. Based partly on his own experiences as a steamboat captain in the Congo in 1890, the story is a complex commentary on the themes of colonialism, racism, and civilization. Some modern critics have called Conrad's representation of Africans in the novel simplistic, or even racist, but his depiction of the cruel and corrupt nature of colonialism contributed to the growing campaign against Leopold's rule in the Congo. In this passage the narrator, Marlow, relates his encounter with African laborers who have literally been worked to death as porters and laborers constructing a railroad through the jungle.

I came upon more pieces of decaying machinery, a stack of rusty rails. To the left a clump of trees made a thick shade, where dark things seemed to stir feebly. I blinked, the path was steep. . . . A slight clinking behind me made me turn my head. Six black men advanced in a file, toiling up the path. They walked erect and slow, balancing small baskets full of earth on their heads, and the clink kept time with their footsteps. Black rags were wound round their loins, and the short ends wagged to and fro like tails. I could see every rib, the joints of their limbs were like knots in a rope; each had an iron collar on his neck, and all were connected together with a chain whose bights swung between them, rhythmically clinking. . . . At last I got under the trees. My purpose was to stroll into the shade for a moment; but no sooner within than it seemed to me I had stepped into the gloomy circle of some Inferno. The rapids were near, and an uninterrupted, uniform, headlong, rushing noise filled the mournful stillness of the grove, where not a breath stirred, not a leaf moved, with a mysterious sound—as though the tearing pace of the launched earth had suddenly become audible.

---

11. Source: Joseph Conrad, *Heart of Darkness* (New York: Penguin Classics, 2007), pp. 18–20.

Black shapes crouched, lay, sat between the trees, leaning against the trunks, clinging to the earth, half coming out, half effaced within the dim light, in all the attitudes of pain, abandonment, and despair. Another mine on the cliff went off, followed by a slight shudder of the soil under my feet. The work was going on. The work! And this was the place where some of the helpers had withdrawn to die.

They were dying slowly—it was very clear. They were not enemies, they were not criminals, they were nothing earthly now—nothing but black shadows of disease and starvation, lying confusedly in the greenish gloom. Brought from all the recesses of the coast in all the legality of time contracts, lost in uncongenial surroundings, fed on unfamiliar food, they sickened, became inefficient, and were then allowed to crawl away and rest. These moribund shapes were free as air—and nearly as thin. I began to distinguish the gleam of eyes under the trees. Then, glancing down, I saw a face near my hand. The black bones reclined at full length with one shoulder against the tree, and slowly the eyelids rose and the sunken eyes looked up at me, enormous and vacant, a kind of blind, white flicker in the depths of the orbs, which died out slowly. The man seemed young—almost a boy—but you know with them it's hard to tell.

DOCUMENT 12

An Englishman's account of the Congo Free State, 1899.[12]

Official reports on the development of the Congo Free State routinely emphasized the humanitarian efforts championed by King Leopold—schools built, missionary stations established, progress made suppressing the slave trade, and the like. However, on the ground the expansion of the rubber regime meant that the state relied increasingly on force to keep order and enforce the collection of rubber. Reports of violence and atrocities became commonplace in the press by the late 1890s, even in King Leopold's favorite paper The Times *of London. The following article, printed in the same year that Conrad published* Heart of Darkness, *is typical of the genre, and clearly ties the escalation of violence in the Congo to the increased demand for rubber.*

A representative of Reuter's Agency has had an interview with Lieutenant Frank J. Andrew, a British subject in the service of the Congo Free State, who has reached England on sick leave from Barumbu, on the Upper Congo, five weeks' journey from the coast, where he held the post of *chef de station*. . . . Asked concerning the fighting which was going on in various parts of the Congo, Lieutenant Andrew said:—"The lower river from the coast to the railway terminus at Leopoldville is quiet and fairly civilized, but once Leopoldville is left a region in which perpetual war reigns is entered. From Leopoldville to the distant shores of Tanganyika the whole interior is the scene of fighting." . . . In answer to questions as to the cause of this absence of order and administration, Lieutenant Andrew replied:—"The origin of the whole thing is not far to seek. In the first place, very few Belgian officers voluntarily go to the Congo. King Leopold makes personal appeals to certain regiments to supply officers, and those who are marched out for the purpose know that it is either a question of going to Africa or forgoing promotion at home. The result is that many parts of the Congo are in charge of non-commissioned officers

12. Source: "An Englishman's Account of Congo State Methods," *The Times* (London), May 26, 1899, p. 6.

quite unsuited for any kind of administrative work; some of whom can scarcely write their own names."

Dealing, in conclusion, with the question of barbarities, Lieutenant Andrew said:—"Personally I saw no actual barbarities as my station was coffee and not rubber producing. But that they exist as badly as ever I have no doubt. They are a direct outcome of the rubber and ivory trade. A lieutenant's pay on the Congo is about £200 per annum, but on a rubber station another £300 can be made on rubber commission. On reaching their posts officers are told how much rubber is expected from each village. If that amount does not come in—no matter for what reason—war is made against that village, and natives are killed, the black soldiers, in order to justify their statements as to the number of dead, afterwards cutting off hands and ears. Was there no rubber—and in a few years (so badly are the vines treated) there will be none—there would be no war."

DOCUMENT 13

The Times of London reports on the Congo rubber trade, 1900.[13]

*At the creation of the Congo Free State ivory was the most
valuable resource available for trade. Steamships and long caravans of porters hauled elephant tusks to the coast for transport to Europe. By the 1890s, however, a much more lucrative
commodity suddenly appeared, rubber. Used for bicycle and
automobile tires, to insulate telegraph wires, and for belts on
industrial machinery, rubber quickly became the most valuable
export from the colony. This report from* The Times *summarizes
the sale of Congo rubber at the Belgian port of Antwerp for
1899. Note the rapid increase of total rubber imported from the
Congo from year to year, and the double-digit price increases
from one year to the next as indicators of the wealth produced
for King Leopold by the rubber regime.*

INDIA RUBBER

ANTWERP, Jan. 12—The first public rubber sale of the year which has
been held this week has proved disappointing in that American buyers
who for some time have been active operators here were conspicuous by
their absence. In spite of this, however, the sale yielded fair results, 181
tons of Congo produce, out of 212¼ tons offered being disposed at an
irregular rise, which averages 15c. per kilo, or 1.8 per cent. Differences of
10c. and more were noted in the price realized by different portions of the
same parcel. The highest price obtained was $10.42 ½c. for red Kassai
and $10.80c. for Lopori and Equateur. Parcels other than Congo received
little attention, and out of 35 tons offered only 11 tons were sold, some
of the prices accepted being as low as 4.5 ½f. per kilo. . . . During the year
1899 2,992½ tons of Congo rubber were imported into Antwerp against
1.734 in 1898, and 410½ tons of other kinds, against 280¼ tons in the
previous year. The total sales here of all kinds during last year amounted

---

13. Source: "India Rubber," *The Times* (London), January 15, 1900, p. 7.

to 3.374 tons against 1.846 in 1898, 1,724 in 1897, 1,665 in 1896, and only 442 in 1895. Prices during the year have risen 6 per cent for red Kassai firsts, 11⅞ per cent for Lopori, 13¼ per cent for Mongalla, 13⅞ per cent for Aruwimi, 14¼ per cent for Equateur and Bussira, 7½ per cent for lower Congo red thimbles, and 12¼ per cent for fine Para. The relatively smaller rise in Kassai compared with other good upper Congos is due to damp packing before shipment, which deterio-rates the quality to some extent.

DOCUMENT 14

In the Rubber Coils, 1906.[14]

Founded in 1841 by the journalist and reformer Henry Mayhew, the British weekly humor magazine Punch *became one of the most widely read and influential periodicals of the Victorian age. The magazine's most famous features were its cartoons—a term first used by the publication to describe a comedic drawing in 1843—which often engaged in sophisticated but biting social and political satire. This cartoon, published at the height of the Congo reform movement, reflected popular opinion on the atrocities committed in Leopold's Congo Free State. It also illustrated awareness of the crucial role played by the rubber trade in the abuses of Leopold's rule.*

14. Source: Linley Sambourne, "In the Rubber Coils (Scene—the Congo 'Free' State)," *Punch*, November 28, 1906. Wikimedia Commons.

IN THE RUBBER COILS.

SCENE—*The Congo "Free" State.*

DOCUMENT 15

An American observer describes the military force of the Congo Free State, 1890s.[15]

Throughout the period of King Leopold's rule much of the controversy surrounding policies of violence and exploitation focused on the actions of the Force Publique, *the army of the Congo Free State. The force consisted of European officers and an African rank and file. During the years of the rubber regime the* Force Publique *became infamous for its use of violence and hostage taking to enforce rubber quotas on crown lands. Edgar Canisius was a young American who served for several years in the Congo as an agent of King Leopold's government, and also for the concessionaire company* Société Anversoise du Commerce au Congo. *Following his time in Africa Canisius wrote a memoir of his experiences, in which he both criticized the administration of the Congo regime and expressed racist attitudes common to whites of the era. In this excerpt from his "A Campaign Amongst Cannibals," he discusses the* Force Publique.

A few additional words concerning the *Force Publique*, or army of the Congo, may here be opportunely introduced. The first recruits to this remarkable agency for spreading "the light of civilization" in Central Africa were taken from the more progressive peoples inhabiting the coast regions, principally British territory. These were Zanzibaris, Abyssinians, Haussas, Sierra Leones, Accras and Elminas. That the British colonial authorities should have permitted the recruiting in British Territory of men intended for the oppression of the native tribes of the Congo was certainly not creditable to the Home Government, which has during recent years so much prided itself on being the "protector" of the black peoples of the earth. Of the many thousand Africans first enlisted for service in the Congo, but few have returned to their native lands, the majority having fallen in the incessant fighting which followed the inception of the "rubber regime."

---

15. Source: Edgar Canisius, "A Campaign Amongst Cannibals," in *The Curse of Central Africa*, by Cpt. Guy Burrows (London: R. A. Everett, 1903), pp. 174–78.

The Congo authorities soon came to the conclusion that one shilling per diem was extravagant payment for soldiers, and as far back as 1886 an effort was made to secure recruits from among the cannibal tribes of the interior. Some Bangalas were sent down to Boma, where they were drilled, and these formed the nucleus of the present army, their pay being about two pence per day. As the state established its authority in other parts of the territory committed to its care, a regular system of recruiting was instituted, each district being called upon to furnish a certain number of conscripts. To explain the *modus operandi* then established and since in vogue requires few words. The *commissaries de district* have orders to see that their quotas are promptly forthcoming, and each naturally enough delegates the duty of recruiting to the *chefs de zone*, who, in their turn, call upon the more subordinate *chefs de poste* to levy upon the local chiefs for the men required. The native chieftain usually makes his selection from the worthless and recalcitrant slaves of the village, who, when they reach the station are promptly placed in the chain, or "collier national" as the Belgians call it, so that they cannot escape. . . .

In some districts the recruits are purchased. From Djabbir, one of the great chiefs of the Uelle district, the State is said to have obtained many hundreds, the price paid being generally one muzzle-loading musket for ten men. It is alleged that Djabbir has many thousands of muskets and a not inconsiderable number of breech-loaders acquired in this way. The traffic is a very simple matter for the dusky potentate, of whom the Belgians seem to stand in much awe; he only has to send his followers to raid the neighboring tribes, and capture as many recruits as the representative of the State may require. With ivory he purchases ammunition from the State posts; for when the sale of firearms to the natives was forbidden, the Government, of course, exempted itself from the operation of the law. . . .

. . . The *Force Publique* has always been conspicuous for its dearth of European officers, and though Belgians still occupy the highest positions and are a considerable majority, many commissions of late have been bestowed upon Italians, Greeks, and Roumanians. According to official returns, the army numbered 14,000, of whom 8,000 were militia, 4,000 native "volunteers," and 2,000 volunteers from the coast. These figures however are somewhat misleading, for in the Congo the term "volunteers" has quite a different meaning to the ordinary. During nearly three years' experience in a State post, I saw but a solitary volunteer present himself for enrollment. . . . From the same post, however, were sent many "volunteers" chained together so they could not escape. . . .

The record of the *Force Publique*, both as a fighting machine and as an instrument for exploiting the natives, goes far to justify the oft-repeated assertion that the African, as a general rule, is not suitable material for the making of a good soldier. That he is frequently unreliable, and likely, on occasion, to prove as dangerous to his employers as the enemy has been proved in the Congo by the revolts in Luluabourg and Kinchassa, and of the troops of Baron Dhanis' expedition to the Nile. . . . It is experience, and not prejudice, which prompts my opinion that no government calling itself civilized should employ African negroes to bear arms for it.

DOCUMENT 16

The Casement Report details abuses in the Congo Free State, 1904.[16]

Roger Casement was an Irish-born member of the British Colonial Service who rose to prominence during the Congo reform movement of the early 1900s. Casement worked with Henry Morton Stanley in the Congo during the 1880s and early 1890s before joining the Colonial Office. While stationed as the British consul in the Congo Free State in 1903, the British government commissioned him to investigate the alleged abuses in the colony. Casement's report, based on extensive interviews with government agents, concession company agents, and Africans, provided evidence to confirm many of the worst allegations. It proved instrumental in advancing the case against King Leopold's regime. He also participated in founding the Congo Reform Association with E. D. Morel and missionary Henry Grattan Guinness. Hailed internationally as a hero for his humanitarian work, Casement's life took a tragic turn in his final years. He became increasingly involved in Irish nationalist politics during the years before World War I. After the war broke out, Casement worked to gain German assistance for an Irish nationalist rebellion and was executed by the British government for treason in 1916.

A careful investigation of the conditions around the lake confirmed the truth of the statements made to me—that the great decrease in population, the dirty and ill-kept towns, and the complete absence of goats, sheep, or fowls—once very plentiful in this country—were to be attributed above all else to the continued effort made during many years to compel the natives to work india-rubber. Large bodies of native troops had formerly been quartered in the district, and the punitive measures undertaken to this end had endured for a considerable period.

---

16. Source: *The Casement Report, Africa No. 1 (1904), Correspondence and Report From His Majesty's Consul at Boma Respecting the Administration of the Independent State of the Congo* (London: Harrison & Sons, 1904).

During the course of these operations there had been much loss of life, accompanied, I fear, by a somewhat general mutilation of the dead as proof that the soldiers had done their duty. Each village I visited around the lake, save that of Q* and one other, had been abandoned by its inhabitants. To some of these villages the people have only just returned; to others they are now only returning. In one I found the bare and burnt poles of what had been dwellings left standing, and at another—that of R*—the people had fled at the approach of my steamer, and despite the loud cries of my native guides on board, nothing could induce them to return, and it was impossible to hold any intercourse with them. At the three succeeding villages I visited beyond R*, in traversing the lake towards the south, the inhabitants all fled at the approach of the steamer, and it was only when they found whose the vessel was that they could be induced to return. . . .

. . . I asked them why they had run away at my approach, and they said, smiling, "We thought you were Bula Matari" (i.e., "men of the Government"). Fear of this kind was formerly unknown on the upper Congo; and in much more out-of-the-way places visited many years ago the people flocked from all sides to greet a white stranger. But today the apparition of a white man's steamer evidently gave the signal for instant flight.

The chief of the P* post told me that a similar alarm reigned almost everywhere in the country behind his station, and that when he went on the most peaceful missions only a few miles from his house the villages were generally emptied of all human beings when he entered them, and it was impossible in the majority of cases to get into touch with the people in their own homes. . . . He gave as an explanation, when I asked for the reason of this fear of the white man, that as these people were great savages, and knew themselves how many crimes they had committed, they doubtless feared that the white man of the Government was coming to punish their misconduct. He added that they had undoubtedly had an "awful past" at the hands of some of the officials who had preceded him in the local administration, and that it would take time for confidence to be restored. Men, he said, still came to him whose hands had been cut off by the Government soldiers during those evil days, and he said there were still many victims of this species of mutilation in the surrounding country. Two cases of the kind came to my actual notice while I was in the lake. One, a young man, both of whose hands had been beaten off with the butt ends of rifles against a tree, the other a young lad of 11 or 12 years of age, whose right hand was cut off at the wrist. This boy described the circumstances of his mutilation, and, in answer to my inquiry, said that although wounded at the time he was perfectly sensible of the severing of his wrist, but lay still fearing that if he moved he would be killed. In both these cases the Government soldiers had been accompanied by white officers whose names were given to me. Of six natives (one a girl, three little boys, one youth, and one old woman) who had been mutilated in this way during the rubber regime, all except one were dead at the date of my visit. The old woman had died at the beginning of this year, and her niece described to me how the act of mutilation in her case had been accomplished. The day I left Lake Mantumba five men whose hands had been cut off came to the village of T* across the lake to see me, but hearing that I had already gone away they returned to their homes. A messenger came in to tell me, and I sent to T* to find them, but they had then dispersed. Three of them subsequently returned, but too late for me to see them. These were some of those, I presume, to whom the official had referred, for they came from the country in the vicinity of the P* station. . . .

With my arrival in the Lulongo River, I was entering one of the most productive rubber districts of the Congo State, where the industry is said to be in a very flourishing condition. . . . [T]he Concession known as the A.B.I.R. . . . has numerous stations, and a staff of fifty-eight Europeans engaged in exploiting the india-rubber industry, with headquarters at Bassankusu. . . . The transport of all goods and agents of the A.B.I.R. Company, immediately these quit the Concession, is carried on exclusively by the steamers of the Congo Government, the freight and passage money obtained being reckoned as part of the public revenue. I have no actual figures giving the annual output of india-rubber from the A.B.I.R. Concession, but it is unquestionably large, and may, in the case of a prosperous year, reach from 600 to 800 tons. The quality of the A.B.I.R. rubber is excellent and it commands generally a high price on the European market, so that the value of its annual yield may probably be estimated at not less than 150,000*l*. The merchandise used by the Company consists of the usual class of Central African barter goods— cotton cloths of different quality, Sheffield cutlery, machetes, beads, and salt. The latter is keenly sought by the natives of all the interior of Africa. There is also a considerable import by the A.B.I.R. Company, I believe, of cap-guns, which are chiefly used in arming the sentinels—termed "forest guards"—who, in considerable numbers, are quartered in the native villages, throughout the Concession to see that the picked men of each town bring in, with regularity, the fixed quantity of pure rubber required of them every fortnight....

The right of the various Concession Companies operating within the Congo State to employ armed men—whether these bear rifles or cap-guns—is regulated by Government enactments, which confer on these commercial Societies what are termed officially "rights of police" ("*droits de police*")....That the extensive use of armed men in the pay of the so-called Trading Societies, or in the service of the Government, as a means to enforce the compliance with demands for india-rubber, had been very general up to a recent date, is not denied by any one I met on the Upper Congo.

In a conversation with a gentleman of experience on this question, our remarks turned upon the condition of the natives. He produced a disused diary, and in it, I found and copied the following entry:—

> M.P. called on us to get out of the rain, and in conversation with M.Q. in presence of myself and R. said: "The only way to get rubber is to fight for it. The natives are paid 35 centimes per kilog., it is claimed, but that includes a large profit on the cloth; the amount of rubber is controlled by the number of guns, and not the number of bales of cloth. The S.A.B. on the Bussira, with 150 guns, gets only 10 tons (rubber) a month; we, the State, at Momboyo, with 130 guns, get 13 tons per month." "So you count by guns?" I asked him. "*Partout*," M.P. said, "Each time the corporal goes out to get rubber cartridges are given to him. He must bring back all not used; and for every one used, he must bring back a right hand." M.P. told me that sometimes they shot a cartridge at an animal in hunting; then they cut off a hand from a living man. As to the extent which this is carried on, he informed me that in six months they, the State, on the Momboyo River, had used 6,000 cartridges, which means that 6,000 people are killed or mutilated. It means more than 6,000, for the people have told me repeatedly that the soldiers kill children with the butt of their guns....

The course of the Lulongo River below Bassakanusu to its junction with the Congo lies outside the limits of the A.B.I.R. Concession, and the region is, I believe, regarded as one of the free-trading districts wherein no exclusive right to the products of the soil is recognized. The only trading-house in this district is one termed the La Lulanga, which has three depots, or factories, along the river bank, the principle of which is at Mampoko. This Company has a small steamer in which its native produce is collected, but the general transport of all its goods, as in the case of the Concession Societies, is performed by Government craft. The La Lulanga does not, as I understand, enjoy the rights of police . . . but it employs a considerable number of armed men equally termed "forest guards." These men are quartered throughout the lower course of the Lulongo River, and I have found that, as with the A.B.I.R., the sole duty they performed was to compel by force the collection of india-rubber or the supplies which each factory needed. As the district in which the La Lulanga Society car-ried on these operations is one that had already been subjected to still more comprehensive handling by two of the large Concession Companies, who only abandoned it when, as one of their agents informed me, it was nearly exhausted, the stock of rubber vines in it today is drawing to an end, and it is only with great difficulty that the natives are able to produce the quantity sufficient to satisfy their local masters. In the course of my dealings with the natives I found that several of the sentries of this Com-pany had quite recently committed gross offences which, until my arrival, appeared to have gone undetected—certainly unpunished. Murder and mutilation were charged against several of them by name by the natives of certain townships close to the headquarters of the Company, who sought me in the hope that I might help them. These people in several cases said that they had not complained elsewhere because they had felt it was use-less. As long as the rubber tax imposed upon them endured in its present compulsory form with the sanction of the authorities, they said it was idle to draw attention to acts which were but incidental to its collection.

The La Lulanga Company, not any more than the A.B.I.R., would seem to have a legal right to levy taxes, but the fact remains that from the natives who supply those two trading Companies with all that they export as well as with their local supplies of food and material, the Congo Government itself requires no contribution to the public revenue. These people, there-fore, must be either legally exempted from supporting the Government of their country, or else a portion of the contributions they make to the A.B.I.R. and Lulanga Companies must be claimed by that Government in lieu of the taxes it is justified in imposing on these districts.

In the case of the A.B.I.R. Society it is said that a portion of the prof-its are paid in to the public revenues of the Congo Government (who hold certain shares in the undertaking), and that these figure annually in the Budget as "*produit de portefeuille*" [products portfolio]. In making this explanation to me, an agent of one of the Upper Congo trading Companies said the term should more correctly be "*produit de porte-fusil*" [products of the rifle], and to judge from the large numbers of armed men I saw employed, the correction was not apposite.

The Concession Companies, I believe, account for the armed men in their service on the ground that their factories and agents must be protected ... but this legitimate need for safeguarding European establishments does not suffice to account for the presence, far from these establishments, of large numbers of armed men quartered throughout the native villages, and who exercise upon their surroundings an influence far from protective. The explanation offered me of this state of things was that, as the "impositions" laid upon the natives were regulated by law, and were calculated on the scale of public labour the Government had a right to require of the people, the collection of these "impositions" had to be strictly enforced. When I pointed out that the profit of this system was not reaped by the Government, but by a commercial Company, and figured in the public returns of that Company's affairs, as well as in the official Government statistics, as the outcome of commercial dealing with the natives, I was informed that the "impositions" were in reality trade, "for as you observe, we pay the natives for the produce they bring in." "But," I observed, "you told me just now that these products did not belong to the natives, but to you, the Concessionaire, who owned the soil; how, then, do you buy from them what is already yours?" "We do not buy the india-rubber. What we pay to the native is a remuneration for his labour in collecting our produce on our land, and bringing it to us."

Since it was thus to the labour of the native alone that the profits of the Company were attributed, I inquired whether he was not protected by contract with his employer; but I was here referred back to the statement that the native performed these services as a public duty required of him by his Government. He was not a contracted labourer at all, but a free man, dwelling in his own home, and was simply acquitting himself of an "imposition" laid upon him by Government, "of which we are but the collectors by right of our Concession." "Your Concession, then, implies," I said, "that you have been conceded not only a certain area of land, but also the people dwelling on that land?" This, however, was not accepted either, and I was assured that the people were absolutely free, and owed no service to anyone but the Government of the country. But there was no explanation that was offered to me that was not contradicted by the next. One said it was a tax, an obligatory burden laid upon the people, such as all Governments have the undoubted right of imposing; but this failed to explain how, if a tax, it came to be collected by the agents of a trading firm, and figured as the income of their trade dealings with the people, still less, how, if it were a tax, it could justly be imposed every week or fortnight in the year, instead of once, or at most, twice a year.

Another asserted that it was clearly legitimate commerce with the natives because these were well paid and very happy. He could not then explain the presence of so many armed men in their midst, or the reason for tying up men, women, and children, and of maintaining in each trading establishment a local prison, termed a "*maison des otages*," wherein recalcitrant native traders endured long periods of confinement.

A third admitted that there was not law on the Congo Statute Book constituting his trading establishment a Government taxing station, and that since the product of his dealings with the natives figured in his Company's balance-sheets as trade, and paid customs duty to the Government on export, and a dividend to the shareholders, and as he himself drew a commission of 2 per cent on his turnover, it must be trade; but this exponent could not explain how, if these operations were purely commercial they rested on a privilege denied to others, for since, as he asserted, the products of his district could neither be worked nor bought by anyone but himself, it was clear they were not merchandise, which, to be merchandise, must be marketable. The summing up of the situation by the majority of those with whom I sought to discuss it was that, in fact, it was forced labour conceived in the true interest of the native, who, if not controlled this way would spend his days in idleness, unprofitable to himself and the general community. The collection of the products of the soil by the more benevolent methods adopted by the Trading Companies was, in any case, preferable to those the Congo Government would itself employ to compel obedience to this law, and therefore if I saw women and children seized as hostages and kept in detention until rubber or other things were brought in, it was better that this should be done by the cap-gun of the "forest guard" than by the Albini armed soldiers of the Government who, if once impelled into a district, would overturn the entire countryside.

No more satisfactory explanation than this outline was anywhere offered me of what I saw in the A.B.I.R. and Lulanga districts. It is true alternatives of excuse with differing interpretations of what I saw were offered me in several quarters, but these were so obviously untrue, that they could not be admitted as having any real relations to the things which came before me.

DOCUMENT 17

African villagers describe the rubber regime, 1904.[17]

*The implementation of the rubber regime created severe dislo-
cations throughout the Congo, as thousands of Congolese fled
their villages to escape rubber collecting. Much of Casement's
report was based on testimony he took from Africans in refugee
villages in the vicinity of Bolobo and Lake Leopold II. This excerpt
illustrates the devastating impact of the demand for rubber upon
entire communities, and how the lack of food and resources
made villages susceptible to disease and famine.*

"I am Moyo. These other two beside me are Waukaki and Mkwabali, all
of us Bangongo. From our country each village had to take twenty loads
of rubber. These loads were as big as this ...." (Producing an empty basket
which came nearly up to the handle of my walking stick.) "That was the
first size. We had to fill that up, but as rubber got scarcer the white man
reduced the amount. We had to take these loads in four times a month."

Q. "How much pay did you get for this?"

A. (Entire audience.) "We got no pay! We got nothing!"

And then Moyo, who I asked again said: —

"Our village got cloth and a little salt, but not the people who did the
work. Our chiefs eat up the cloth; the workers got nothing. The pay was
a fathom of cloth and a little salt for every big basket full, but it was
given to the Chief, never to the men. It used to take ten days to get the
twenty baskets of rubber—we were always in the forest and then when
we were late we were killed. We had to go further and further into the
forest to find the rubber vines, to go without food, and our women had to
give up cultivating fields and gardens. Then we starved. Wild beasts—the
leopards—killed some of us when were working away in the forest, and
others got lost or died from exposure and starvation, and we begged the
white men to leave us alone, saying we could get no more rubber, but the
white men and their soldiers said: 'Go! You are only beasts yourselves,
you are *nyama* (meat).' We tried, always to go further into the forest, and

17. Source: Cited in R. Anstey, "The Congo Rubber Atrocities—A Case Study," *African
Historical Studies* IV, no. 1 (1971), pp. 63–64.

when we failed and our rubber was short, the soldiers came to our towns and killed us. Many were shot, some had their ears cut off; others were tied up with ropes around their necks and bodies taken away. The white men sometimes at the posts did not know of the bad things the soldiers did to us, but it was the white men who sent the soldiers to punish us for not bringing in enough rubber."

DOCUMENT 18

E. D. Morel critiques imperialism and describes the Leopoldian system, 1920.[18]

Edmund Dene Morel rose to prominence as the principal leader of the Congo reform movement. In 1904 the former shipping company agent turned journalist and activist founded the Congo Reform Association with Roger Casement and missionary Henry Grattan Guinness. Following the successful campaign to oust King Leopold as sovereign of the Congo Free State, Morel's views on politics and imperialism continued to evolve in a more radical direction. He was a vocal pacifist during World War I, and became a more outspoken critic of imperialism in general. In these excerpts from The Black Man's Burden: The White Man in Africa from the Fifteenth Century to World War I, *Morel questions the nationalist and humanitarian underpinnings of imperialism, making an explicit counterargument to Rudyard Kipling's famous poem "The White Man's Burden" (1899). He also offers a succinct summary of the Leopoldian system in the Congo Free State.*

The bard of a modern Imperialism has sung of the White Man's burden.

The notes strike the granite surface of racial pride and fling back echoes which reverberate through the corridors of history, exultant, stirring the blood with memories of heroic adventure, deeds of desperate daring, ploughing of unknown seas, vistas of mysterious continents, perils affronted and overcome, obstacles triumphantly surmounted. . . .

What of that other burden, not our own self-imposed one which national and racial vanity may well overstress; but the burden we have laid on others in the process of assuming ours; the burden which others are bearing now because of us? . . .

These contemplations are not a fit theme for lyrical outpourings. These questions are unbidden guests at the banquet of self-laudation. They excite no public plaudits, arise no patriotic enthusiasms, pander to no racial conceits. They typify the skeleton at the imperial feast.

---

18. Source: E. D. Morel, *The Black Man's Burden: The White Man in Africa from the Fifteenth Century to World War I* (New York, B. W. Huebsch: 1920), pp. 3–4, 7–9, 115–19.

But this is a time of searching inquiry for the white races; of probing scrutiny into both past and present; of introspection in every branch of human endeavour.

And these questions must be asked. They must be confronted in the fullness of their import, in the utmost significance of their implications—and they must be answered. . . .

It is with the peoples of Africa, then, that our inquiry is concerned. It is they who carry the "Black Man's" burden. They have not withered away before the white man's *occupation*. . . . In hewing out for himself a fixed abode in Africa, the white man has massacred the African in heaps. The African has survived, and it is well for the white settlers that he has.

In the process of imposing his political domination over the African, the white man has carved broad and bloody avenues from one end of Africa to the other. The African has resisted and persisted.

For three centuries the white man seized and enslaved millions of Africans and transported them, with every circumstance of ferocious cruelty, across the seas. Still the African survived and, in his land of exile, multiplied exceedingly.

But what the partial occupation of his soil by the white man has failed to do; what the mapping out of European political "spheres of influence" has failed to do; what the maxim and rifle has failed to do; what the slave gang, labour in the bowels of the earth and lash, have failed to do; what imported measles, smallpox and syphilis have failed to do; what even the oversea [sic] slave trade failed to do, the power of modern capitalistic exploitation, assisted by modern engines of destruction, may yet succeed in accomplishing.

For from the evils of the latter, scientifically applied and enforced, there is no escape for the African. Its destructive effects are not spasmodic: they are permanent. In its permanence resides its fatal consequences. It kills not the body merely, but the soul. It breaks the spirit. It attacks the African at every turn, from every point of vantage. It wreaks his polity, uproots him from the land, invades his family life, destroys his natural pursuits and occupations, enslaves him in his own home. . . .

Thus the African is really helpless against the material gods of the white man, as embodied in the trinity of imperialism, capitalistic-exploitation, and militarism. If the white man retains these gods and if he insists upon making the African worship them as assiduously as he has done himself, the African will go the way of the Red Indian, the Amerindian, the Carib, the Guanche, the aboriginal Australian, and many more. And this would be at once a crime of enormous magnitude, and a world disaster. . . .

From 1891 until 1912, the paramount object of European rule in the Congo was the pillaging of its natural wealth to enrich private interests in Belgium. To achieve this end a specific, well-defined System was thought out in Brussels and applied in the Congo. Its essential features were known to the Belgian Government from 1898 onwards. They were defended in principle, and their effects denied, by successive Belgian ministries, some of whose members were actively concerned in the working of the System, and even personal beneficiaries from it . . . although the Belgian Government did not govern the Congo, and, while apologizing for and acclaiming the methods of administration there pursued, washed its hands of responsibility for the actions of what it termed "a foreign state." . . .

In the nature of the case, the execution of this Policy took some years before it could become really effective and systematic. . . .

. . . A native army was the prerequisite. The five years which preceded the Edicts of 1891–92 were employed in raising the nucleus of a force of 5,000. It was successively increased to nearly 20,000 apart from the many thousands of "irregulars" employed by the Concessionaire Companies. This force was amply sufficient for the purpose, for a single native soldier armed with a rifle and with a plentiful supply of ball cartridge can terrorize a village. . . . A systematic warfare upon the women and children would prove an excellent means of pressure. They would be converted into "hostages" for the good behaviour, in rubber collecting, of the men. "Hostage houses" would become an institution in the Congo. But in certain parts of the Congo the rubber-vine did not grow. This peculiarity of nature was, in one way, all to the good. For the army of Officials and native soldiers, with their wives, and concubines, and camp followers generally required feeding. The non-rubber producing districts should feed them. Fishing tribes would be "taxed" in fish; agricultural tribes in foodstuffs. In this case, too, the women and children would answer for the men. Frequent military expeditions would probably be an unfortunate necessity. Such expeditions would demand in every case hundreds of carriers for the transport of loads, ammunition, and general impedimenta. Here again, was an excellent school in which this idle people could learn the dignity of labour. The whole territory would thus become a busy hive of human activities, continuously and usefully engaged for the benefit of the "owners" of the soil thousands of miles away, and their crowned Head, whose intention, proclaimed on repeated occasions to an admiring world, was the "moral and material regeneration" of the natives of the Congo.

Such was the Leopoldian "System," briefly epitomized.

DOCUMENT 19

Mark Twain's *King Leopold's Soliloquy*, 1905.[19]

As the Congo reform campaign drew significant international interest during the first decade of the twentieth century several prominent literary figures participated. The best-known work on the Congo is clearly Joseph Conrad's Heart of Darkness *(Document 11). However, Mark Twain and Arthur Conan Doyle were other literary giants who contributed their talents to the anti-Leopold movement. Twain published his political satire* King Leopold's Soliloquy *in 1905, promising to donate all proceeds from the pamphlet to "furthering effort for relief of the people of the Congo State." The work features a monologue by a caricature of the king who defends his humanitarian efforts and vehemently castigates his critics, including missionaries and the international press.*

[*Throws down pamphlets which he has been reading. Excitedly combs his flowing spread of whiskers with his fingers; pounds the table with his fists; lets off brisk volleys of unsanctified language at brief intervals, repentantly drooping his head, between volleys, and kissing the Louis XI crucifix hanging from his neck, accompanying the kisses with mumbled apologies; presently rises, flushed and perspiring, and walks the floor, gesticulating.*]

_____ _____!! _____ _____!! If I had them by the throat! [*Hastily kisses the crucifix, and mumbles*] In these twenty years I have spent millions to keep the press of the two hemispheres quiet, and still these leaks keep on occurring. I have spent other millions on religion and art, and what do I get for it? Nothing. Not a compliment. These generosities are studiously ignored, in print. In print I get nothing but slanders, and slanders on top of slanders! Grant them true, what of it? They are slanders all the same, when uttered against a king.

Miscreants—they are telling *everything*! Oh, everything: how I went pilgrimming among the Powers in tears, with my mouth full of Bible and my pelt oozing piety at every pore, and implored them to place the vast

19. Source: Mark Twain, *King Leopold's Soliloquy* (Boston: P. R. Warren, 1906), pp. 5–9.

and rich and populous Congo Free State in trust in my hands as their agent, so that I might root out slavery and stop the slave raids, and lift up those twenty-five millions of gentle and harmless blacks out of darkness into light, the light of our blessed Redeemer, the light that makes glorious our noble civilization—lift them up and dry their tears and fill their bruised hearts with joy and gratitude—lift them up and make them comprehend that they were no longer outcasts and forsaken, but our very brothers in Christ; how America and thirteen great European states wept in sympathy with me, and were persuaded; how their representatives met in convention in Berlin and made me Head Foreman and Superintendent of the Congo State, and drafted out my powers and limitations, carefully guarding the persons and liberties and properties of the natives against hurt and harm; forbidding whiskey traffic and gun traffic; providing courts of justice; making commerce free and fetterless to the merchants and traders of all nations, and welcoming and safe-guarding all missionaries of all creeds and denominations. They have told how I planned and prepared my establishment and selected my horde of officials—"pals" and "pimps" of mine, "unspeakable Belgians" every one—and hoisted my flag, and "took in" a President of the United States, and got him to be the first to recognize it and salute it. Oh, well, let them blackguard me if they like; it is a deep satisfaction to me to remember that I was a shade too smart for that nation that thinks itself so smart. Yes, I certainly did bunco a Yankee—as those people phrase it. Pirate flag? Let them call it so—perhaps it is. All the same, *they were the first to salute it.*

These meddlesome American missionaries! these frank British consuls! these blabbing Belgian-born traitor officials!—those tiresome parrots are always talking, always telling. They have told how for twenty years I have ruled the Congo State not as a trustee of the Powers, an agent, a subordinate, a foreman, but as a sovereign—sovereign over a fruitful domain four times as large as the German Empire—sovereign absolute, irresponsible, above all law; trampling the Berlin-made Congo charter under foot; barring out all foreign traders but myself; restricting commerce to myself, through concessionaires who are my creatures and confederates; seizing and holding the State as my personal property, the whole of its vast revenues as my private "swag"—mine, solely mine—claiming and holding its millions of people as my private property, my serfs, my slaves; their labor mine, with or without wage; the food they raise not their property but mine; the rubber, the ivory and all the other riches of the land mine—mine solely—and gathered for me by the men, the women and the little children under compulsion of lash and bullet, fire, starvation, mutilation and the halter.

These pests!—it is as I say, they have kept back nothing! They have revealed these and yet other details which shame should have kept them silent about, since they were exposures of a king, a sacred personage and immune from reproach, by right of his selection and appointment to his great office by God himself; a king whose acts cannot be criticized without blasphemy, since God has observed them from the beginning and has manifested no dissatisfaction with them, nor shown disapproval of them, nor hampered nor interrupted them in any way. By this sign I recognize his approval of what I have done; his cordial and glad approval, I am sure I may say.

Blest, crowned, beatified with this great reward, this golden reward, this unspeakably precious reward, why should I care for men's cursing and revilings of me?

DOCUMENT 20

A British diplomat compares British rule favorably to the government of the Congo Free State, 1903.[20]

As controversy surrounding the abuses of the Congo Free State administration turned into an international scandal, King Leopold's rule became a useful foil against which established colonial powers could downplay exploitation in their own empires. In this document the Earl of Cromer, the British consul-general of Egypt, reports to the foreign secretary on his tour of the Upper Nile region of the Southern Sudan. The western bank of the river, known as the Lado Enclave, was ruled by the Congo Free State, while the eastern bank was British. Note how Cromer repeatedly casts the Belgian administration in a negative light in contrast to the positive impact of British rule.

Earl of Cromer to the Marquis of Landsdowne. (Received February 9)
On the Nile, near Kiro, January 21, 1903

I HAVE just visited the Belgian stations of Kiro and Lado, as also the station of Gondokoro in the Uganda Protectorate.

Your Lordship may like to receive some remarks on the impressions I derived as regards the Belgian positions on the Upper Nile. . . .

From the point of view of appearance, the two Belgian stations contrast favourably with any of the Soudanese stations on the Nile, and still more favourably with Gondokoro in the Uganda Protectorate. The principal dwelling-houses are of brick. They seem to be well-built. These stations are kept scrupulously clean. The troops are well-housed. Flourishing gardens have been created. I counted the graves of nine Europeans at Kiro, all of whom died of fever, but I am informed that the health of the place is now greatly improved.

I had heard so many and such contradictory accounts of the Belgian Administration that I was very desirous of ascertaining some concise and definite evidence on this subject. During a hurried visit, and with

---

20. Source: *Accounts and Papers, Colonies and British Possessions—Africa, Session 2 February, 1904–15 August, 1904*, vol. LXII (London: Harrison and Sons, 1904), pp. 1–2.

opportunities of observation confined to the banks of the river, I scarcely anticipated that I should be able to arrive at any independent opinion on the point at issue. I saw and heard, however, quite enough to gain an insight into the spirit which pervades the Administration.

It must be remembered that the 1,100 miles of country which I traversed between Khartoum and Gondokoro has, until recently, been the prey of slave-dealers, Egyptian Pashas, and dervishes. Under the circumstances, it might well have been expected that much time would be required to inspire confidence in the intentions of the new Government. It is, however, certain that, with the exception of a portion of the Nuer tribe, who live in a very remote region on the upper waters of the Sobat, confidence has been completely established in those districts which are under British rule. Except in the uninhabitable "Sudd" region, numerous villages are dotted along the banks of the river. The people, far from flying at the approach of white men as was formerly the case, run along the banks, making signs for the steamer to stop. It is clear that the Baris, Shilluks, and Dinkas place the utmost trust and confidence in the British officers with whom they are brought in contact.... They flock into the Settlements without fear; and if, as often happens, they will not work, it is merely because they are lazy and have few wants, not because they entertain doubt that they will be paid for working. . . .

The contrast when once Congolese territory is entered is remarkable. . . . The proper left, or western, bank of the river is Belgian. . . . I cannot say that I had an opportunity of seeing a full 80 miles of Belgian territory. At the same time, I saw a good deal, and I noticed that, whereas there were numerous villages and huts on the eastern bank and the islands, on the Belgian side not a sign of a village existed. Indeed, I do not think that any one of our party saw a single human being in Belgian territory, except that Belgian officers and men and the wives and children of the latter. Moreover, not a single native was to be seen at either Kiro or Lado. . . .

The reason of all this is obvious enough. The Belgians are disliked. The people fly from them, and it is no wonder they should do so, for I am informed that the soldiers are allowed full liberty to plunder, and that payments are rarely made for supplies. The British officers wander, practically alone, over most parts of the country, either on tours of inspection or shooting expeditions. I understand that no Belgian officer can move outside the settlements without a strong guard.

It appears to me that the facts which I have stated above afford amply sufficient evidence of the spirit which animates the Belgian Administration, if, indeed, Administration it can be called. The Government, so far as I could judge, is conducted almost exclusively on commercial principles, and, even judged by that standard, it would appear that these principles are somewhat short-sighted.

DOCUMENT 21

King Leopold defends himself in the American press, 1906.[21]

During the early years of the twentieth century, King Leopold engaged in a significant campaign to discredit and push back against the many critics of his Congo regime. This article presents an interview with the king published in numerous American newspapers, including The New York Times. *Notice how the king repeatedly seeks to emphasize humanitarian and development policies in the Congo Free State, while downplaying his connections to profits from the enterprises there. Both of these are claims that the historical record shows to be demonstrably untrue. Note also what seems to be his direct reference to the* Punch *cartoon "In the Rubber Coils" (Document 14), which appeared in print just two weeks prior to the publication of this interview.*

KING LEOPOLD DENIES CHARGES AGAINST HIM
Is Poorer Instead of Richer Because of the Congo, He Says.
NOT A MONSTER, EITHER
May Have Been Misjudgment and Even Crime in the African Region, but no Countenanced Atrocities

Brussels, Belgium, Dec. 10—In an interview given personally to-day to the correspondent of the Publishers' Press, King Leopold of Belgium denied categorically the reports which have been circulated so widely of atrocities practiced in the Congo. . . .

"Then it is not true that atrocious conditions exist in the Congo region?" he was asked.

"Of course not. People should credit us with common sense, even if they will not allow that humanity exists outside their own country. It would be absurd for us to mistreat the blacks because no State prospers unless the population is happy and increasing. America knows perhaps,

21. Source: "King Leopold Denies Charges Against Him," *The New York Times*, Dec. 11, 1906.

better than any country, how true this is. Many of the people maligning us are doing so from interested motives. It seems a new trade has arisen in the world, that of calumniation. There are those who make their living by forming associations to protest against everything under heaven. . . .

"I do not deny there have been cases of misjudgment on the part of Congo officials. Most likely cruelties, even crimes have been committed. There have been a number of convictions before Congo tribunals for these offenses. I do deny that every effort as far as possible has not been made to stop the ill treatment of natives not only by white people, but by natives themselves." . . .

Leopold dwelt at some length on what has been accomplished in the Congo, saying: "We have been fortunate in reducing smallpox in Central Africa by the introduction of vaccine. We have stopped the Congo slave trade and prohibited alcohol from entering the country, but steamers on the rivers have built and are building railways and introduced the telegraph. Now we are sending out motor cars . . . .

"It is asserted you are financially interested in the Congo and make a huge fortune there yearly. Is this so?"

Leopold replied: "It is absolutely false. I am the ruler of the Congo, but the prosperity of the country no more affects me financially than the prosperity of America increased the means of President Roosevelt. I have not one cent invested in Congo industries and I have not received any salary as Congo Executive in the past twenty-two years. In no shape or form have I bettered myself financially through my relationship with the Congo . . . .

"I know there are persons so constituted that they are unable to appreciate such a statement. They believe readily enough, however, false charges that I am rolling in wealth at the expense of dying natives. They see me as a boa constrictor, squeezing the life out of the blacks in order to put gold in my purse." . . . "I am not a businessman. I am a ruler, anxious only for the welfare of my subjects. It is more to me than money to a miser for me to know my work in the Congo has not been vainly spent. From a wild African forest, inhabited by cannibals, the Congo is developed wonderfully, its revenues increasing from nothing to $10,000,000 annually. But what has been accomplished is nothing to what will be. There is fabulous wealth in the country. I am making every effort to see that it is properly developed. I cannot conceive anything that will give a greater return than planting rubber trees there. Rubber sells for $2,000 a ton, and the Congo is the natural rubber region of the world.

"To see this development of the Congo is my reward."

DOCUMENT 22

Allies of King Leopold defend the Congo Free State against accusations of abuse, 1891 and 1905.[22]

King Leopold also used hired agents of the Belgian and Congo governments to respond to critics, and maintained a network of paid defenders of the Congo Free State throughout Europe and the United States. These documents provide two examples. In the first, Alfred LeGhait, a Belgian diplomat stationed in the United States, writes to the New York Herald *after it had published a summary of the accusations in George Washington Williams'* Open Letter *(Document 9). In the second, James Gustavus Whiteley, a Baltimore-based lawyer, author, and "consul" of the Congo Free State to the United States, writes a review in* The New York Times *of a book defending the state and the king. Whiteley praises the work as an objective and neutral account of the Congo, without revealing that he, and its author, Henry Wellington Wack, were on King Leopold's payroll.*

New York Herald (1891):

I find in today's edition of your esteemed newspaper an article summarizing a publication of Colonel Williams on the Congo Free State.

I am persuaded that a newspaper which has taken such an important part in the development of civilization in Africa . . . cannot believe for an instant the malevolent inventions of Mr. Williams. I am surprised to see his claims given protection in the columns of such a publication without the reprobation and the commentaries that they merited, which can only inspire him.

The civilizing work of King Leopold is too dignified and respectable; the end and the means being too high as the benefits are already

---

22. Source: Correspondence of Baron Lambermont, Congo (72-270), John Hope Franklin Papers/W10/Books—George Washington Williams, Duke University Rubenstein Library and University Archives [Research Materials], Durham, NC; and "The Congo Free State," *The New York Times*, March 4, 1905.

universally appreciated for me to need to defend against the low false accusations that have been made, but desiring to cooperate with Mr. Stanley to not leave the public opinion of your large and agreeable country under the false impression it could after reading this pamphlet, I want to say to you I associate myself entirely with the declarations made on this subject by the illustrious American explorer, as they were reported in your previously cited article, and that I have good reasons for confirming them.

I do not doubt on the other hand that with the numerous and excellent information at your disposal you will subsequently present the situation of the Congo in its true light, and as I highly estimate your just and impartial newspaper, I hope you will take this into account.

Wishing, etc.

A. LeGhait

March 4, 1905

THE CONGO FREE STATE

Mr. Henry Wellington Wack's Study of the Social, Political, and Economic Aspects of Belgian Rule in Central Africa

If anybody thirsts after knowledge about the Congo in these days it's his own fault if he doesn't get it. He can get true stories or false ones, just as he pleases, the latter, like false diamonds, being much cheaper and more numerous. . . .

Up to a few years ago Americans got along very well without knowing anything at all about the Congo. They were ignorant, but they were blissful, and although the United States is the greatest rubber-using country in the world, and buys the larger part of the Congo rubber crop, the American public left all that business to the Rubber Trust and did not trouble its head about what was going on in Central Africa. But some people have knowledge thrust upon them. Two or three American missionaries and some of our British cousins have insisted upon the United States taking an interest in their campaign for the overthrow of King Leopold's Government in Africa. . . .

Mr. Wack gives an account of the anti-Congo campaign as carried on here and in England. He seems to have formed an uncomplimentary opinion of some of the missionaries engaged in it; but it must be remembered that these men are not representative of the missionary body. The great majority of missionaries on the Congo praise the rule of King Leopold in Africa, and out of 600 missionaries, only about a score have complained of his administration....

The adversaries of the Congo accuse King Leopold's Government of maladministration. A Government is to be judged not by theories but by actual results ... and Mr. Wack gives the present conditions in the Congo—the results obtained—as well as steps by which those results were reached. He traces the history of the state from the period thirty years ago ... and shows what vast changes have taken place in that short space under King Leopold. He tells what the country was then and what it is now. Then this great territory of nearly a million square miles was a scene of barbarism, cannibalism, and inter-tribal wars—but the chief curse of the country consisted in the Arab slave raids, wherein it is estimated a hundred thousand natives were killed or carried off every year. Mr. Wack gives in some detail an account of the brave campaigns of the Belgians which resulted in the absolute suppression of these raids. It was a great and noble work, which cleared the way for Christianity and civilization. But that part of King Leopold's task is now done—and, by some ungrateful souls, almost forgotten....

The book continues many interesting photographs of substantial bridges, of railways, of schools of carpentry and weaving, of the Government orphan asylums, of the Public Printing office with natives at the press, of well-built brick churches, of mission stations, and of hospitals. According to recent statistics there are over 500 schools, and more than 1,200 pieces of land are in use for religious purposes....

To plant the standard of civilization on the soil of Central Africa has for years been the steadfast purpose of the King. The development of the Congo was his idea, and he has spared neither time nor thought nor money to realize his ideal. In view of the recent criticism of his administration by a few persons who have been heard for their much speaking rather than on account of their worth, his Majesty has sent a royal commission to examine conditions out there and to suggest any improvements that may be made.... They have full powers to investigate everything, and the investigation is to be public so that foreign powers may, if they wish, watch the proceedings. This thing will not be done in a corner, and the character of the men employed insures a fair and full investigation.

DOCUMENT 23

Commission of Inquiry confirms abusive practices in the Congo Free State, 1906.[23]

As international pressure on King Leopold mounted, he was forced to address the accusations of violence in the Congo Free State. In 1906 the king appointed a Commission of Inquiry, consisting of three judges—one Belgian, one Swiss, and one Italian—to investigate the administration of the colony. Leopold expected that the commission would provide evidence to absolve him, as investigations in the 1890s had done. However, after conducting interviews with Africans throughout the colony for several months the commissioners accumulated overwhelming evidence of the abuses committed during the rubber regime. The evidence was so compelling the Belgian government kept the transcripts of testimony classified as a state secret for more than seventy-five years. The summary of the evidence published by the commission was damaging enough to force the king to begin negotiations for transferring control over the colony to the Belgian government. The text below includes excerpts from the commission's report published by the Congo Reform Association.

Appropriation of Land and Products

"In default of a legal definition, it seems to have been generally admitted on the Congo that lands considered as being occupied by the natives are exclusively the portions of territory upon which they have established their villages or raised their plantations....

"It has even been admitted that on the land occupied by them, the natives cannot dispose of the produce of the soil except to the extent in which they did so before the constitution of the State....

"As the greater portion of the land in the Congo is not under cultivation, this interpretation concedes to the State a right of absolute and

---

23. Source: *The Findings of King Leopold's Commission/Commission chargée de faire et enquête les territoires de l'État du Congo* (Boston: Congo Reform Association, 1906).

exclusive ownership over virtually the whole of the land, with this consequence: that it can dispose—itself and solely—of all the products of the soil; prosecute as a poacher anyone who takes from that land the least of its fruits, or as a receiver of stolen goods anyone who receives such fruit."

The Native . . . Possesses Nothing

"There are no native reserves and, apart from the rough plantations which barely suffice to feed the natives themselves and to supply the stations, all the fruits of the soil are considered as the property of the State or of the concessionaire societies. Thus, although the freedom of trade is formally recognized by law, the native does not own, in many places, the objects which constitute trade."

All Products Claimed by the State

"The labor tax is the only impost possible on the Congo, because the native as a general rule possesses nothing beyond his hut, his weapons and a few plantations strictly necessary for his subsistence.

"It is useful to point out that according to the *arête* of 5th October, 1889, 'any person can use his weapons to defend his life or property threatened by one or several elephants. If the adoption of such measures lead to the capture, or the death of the elephant, the animal must be handed over to the District Commissioner.'"

Rubber Collection

"This circumstance (exhaustion of the rubber) explains the repugnance of the native for rubber work which, in itself, is not particularly painful. In the majority of cases the native must go one or two days' march every fortnight, until he arrives at that part of the forest where the rubber vines can be met within a certain degree of abundance. There the collector passes a number of days in a miserable existence. He has to build himself an impoverished shelter, which cannot, obviously, replace his hut. He has not the food to which he is accustomed. He is deprived of his wife, exposed to the inclemencies of the weather and the attacks of wild beasts. When once he has collected the rubber he must bring it to the State Station or to that of the Company, and only then can he return to his village, where he can sojourn for barely more than two or three days, because the next demand is upon him."

"OFFICIALS HAVE FLOGGED RUBBER COLLECTORS"
The Rule of Force

"The only legal means at the disposal of the State, for compelling the native to work, is by ordaining a labor-tax.

"As soon as the territory near to the villages was exhausted, and, consequently, the labor of the native become more painful, force was alone able to conquer the apathy of the native.

"The disinclination of the negro for all work; his particular antipathy to gathering rubber, have made force a necessity.

"The native only understands, only respects, force: He confounds it with justice. The State must be able to ensure the triumph of law, and consequently force the native to work.

"From what precedes, it may be concluded, we think, that everywhere on the Congo, notwithstanding certain appearances to the contrary, the native only collects rubber under the influence of force directly or indirectly exercised.

"Very often, then, in order to secure workmen, force has been used and chiefs have been compelled to furnish workers as they have furnished soldiers.

"Until recently this compulsion has been exerted in divers ways, such as carrying away of hostages, imprisonment of chiefs, stationing sentinels or overseers, fines and armed expeditions.

"Officials in charge of stations, arrogating to themselves a right which never belonged to them, have flogged rubber collectors who have not completely satisfied the requirements demanded of them. Some have even committed outrages, which is established by the judgments of the Courts. Natives instructed to supervise the prisoners have been guilty of acts of violence towards them, often of the gravest character."

Flogging with the *Chicotte*

"The blacks employed by the State should accept, along with the other conditions of their contract, the disciplinary punishments which practically are the same as apply to the soldiers. The use of the *chicotte* is the most frequent form of punishment. The rules indicate fifty strokes as the maximum, and not more than twenty-five may be given an offender in any one day. In case of a wound being caused, or fainting, the strokes must cease immediately.

"Despite the provisions of the law as to the use of the *chicotte*, violations at times occur, either in its too frequent use for minor offenses or in exceeding the prescribed number of strokes."

The Hostage System

"When the rubber fell short, the agents arrested the chief of the village, or seized as hostages some of the inhabitants, often women, taken haphazard . . . and kept them sometimes for several months.

"We were, it is true, assured that the prisoners were not badly treated, that excessive labors were not imposed upon them. We have been told that the lot of the women prisoners was not more painful than the existence of beasts of burden to which native custom subjects them. Nevertheless it is undeniable that imprisonment has often been aggravated by its accompanying circumstances.

"We were informed that the houses of detention were often in a very bad state, that the prisoners were insufficiently fed, and that the death rate amongst them was high."

DOCUMENT 24

The Lejeune Report documents the mistreatment of African workers in the Belgian Congo, 1923.[24]

In 1908 King Leopold turned over control of the Congo Free State to the Belgian government. The administration of the newly christened Belgian Congo sought to enact reforms to end the abuses, but the territory remained a significant source of valuable tropical raw materials. The colonial government continued to grant large concessions to companies for the extraction and exploitation of these resources. One of the most prominent examples was the Huileries du Congo Belges (HCB), established by British industrialist William Lever to produce palm oil used for the manufacturing of soap by his company, Lever Brothers. Laborers on Lever's palm oil plantations, many of them migrants from other regions of the Congo, faced significant dangers and hardships. The following report compiled by Dr. Emile Lejeune, a medical officer for the Congo-Kasai province, documented the difficult conditions faced by these workers.

In Leverville there is a brick-built camp, which would be good if there were latrines, kitchens and a rubbish pit, and if it were fenced in, cleared of brushwood and regularly whitewashed. Besides, this camp is only large enough for a very small fraction of the workers currently at post.

I have seen the camp of the imported Yanzi. The camp consists of straw houses in which from 10 to 20 men sleep in cramped conditions, on pallets upon which 7 or 8 at the most should be accommodated. The camp is in reality little better than a simple night shelter of poor quality.

The workers living in this camp, 400 in number, have to carry all their valuables with them when they go off to work, for nothing can be locked up. They therefore set out in the morning, around six o'clock, with their sacks and without having eaten. They get THE MEAL at midday, and return in the evening. They have the whole night to chat and to sleep, but nothing to get their teeth into. If they came with their wife, they would

---

24. Source: Cited in Jules Marchal, *Lord Leverhulme's Ghosts* (New York: Verso, 2008), pp. 31–35.

not be given any suitable accommodation. Finally, newcomers often have no shelter, and have to fend for themselves. One may readily understand how it is that, given such conditions, they refuse, after a first stint of three months, to re-enlist. . . .

Rations, accommodation and clothing are inadequate, and on each count the company is to blame . . . the imported workers, who are single, cannot do the work that is asked of them and still remain healthy under existing conditions. . . . Personally, if I were an administrator, I would not send a single worker to the company. . . .

To sum up, I have found things to be in a deplorable state, and I have been deeply disillusioned by the flagrant practical shortcomings of the HCB's medical service so far as the treatment of blacks in Leverville and Kwenge is concerned.

DOCUMENT 25

King Baudouin I of Belgium and Patrice Lumumba give speeches on the independence of the Congo, 1960.[25]

After several years of struggle the Congolese people achieved independence from Belgium on June 30, 1960. The day was celebrated with a series of public celebrations and official ceremonies. King Baudouin I, President Joseph Kasavubu, and Prime Minister Patrice Lumumba gave speeches to mark the occasion of the formal declaration of independence. The king's speech framed the moment as the culmination of the beneficent and humanitarian project launched by Leopold II in 1885, while Lumumba's speech acknowledged the struggle of the Congolese against imperialist oppression. In these excerpts from the two speeches note the contested and contrasting memories and meanings given to the legacy of colonialism by the colonizer and the colonized.

King Baudouin I

The independence of the Congo is the culmination of a work conceived by the genius of King Leopold II, undertaken by him with tenacious courage and continued with perseverance by Belgium. It marks an hour in the destinies, not only of the Congo itself, but, I do not hesitate to say it, the whole of Africa.

When Leopold II undertook the great work which today finds its culmination, it was not as a conqueror but as a civilizer. . . .

The Congo, since its foundation, has opened its borders to international traffic, without ever having a monopoly in Belgium's exclusive interest. . . .

The Congo was endowed with railways, roads, sea and air lines which by bringing your people in contact with each other, united them and extended the country to the dimensions of the world. . . .

25. Source: Centre de Recherche et d'Information Socio-Politiques (CRISP), *Congo, 1960: Documents belges et africains* (Brussels: 1961), pp. 318–20, 323.

Henceforth Belgium and Congo stand side by side as two sovereign nations, linked by friendship and dedication to help one another. We are now handing over to you all of the administrative, economic, technical, social services and judicial organizations without which a modern state is not viable. Belgian agents also stand ready to bring you loyal and enlightened collaboration.

Congolese people,

My country and I recognize with joy and emotion the Congo's accession on June 30, 1960, in full accord and friendship with Belgium, to independence and international sovereignty.

May God protect the Congo!

Patrice Lumumba

Men and Women of the Congo,

Fighters for independence now victorious

I greet you on behalf of the Congolese government. . . .

For this independence of the Congo, if it is proclaimed today in agreement with Belgium, an amicable country with which we stand as an equal, no Congolese worthy of the name can ever forget that it was won by struggle, an ardent and idealistic struggle, in which we were spared neither privation nor suffering, and for which we sacrificed our strength and our blood.

We are proud of this struggle, which was fought with tears, and fire, and blood to the very depths of our being, for it was a noble and just struggle, an indispensable struggle to end the humility of slavery imposed upon us by force. . . .

We have known the ironies, insults, and blows that endured morning, noon, and night, because we are negroes.

We have known our lands to be despoiled in the name of allegedly legal texts that recognized only might is right.

Who will forget the shootings in which so many of our brethren perished, the dungeons into which they were brutally thrown for refusing to submit to a regime of injustice and oppression?

All of these things, my brothers, we have endured. . . .

The Republic of Congo has been proclaimed, and our nation is now in the hands of its own children.

Together my brothers and sisters, we will begin a new struggle, a sublime struggle to lead our nation to peace, prosperity, and greatness.

We will establish together social justice and ensure that everyone receives a just remuneration for his labor.

We will show the world what the black man can do when he works in freedom, and we are going to make the Congo the pride of all of Africa.

We will make our rule, not the peace of guns and bayonets, but the peace of hearts and good will.

The independence of the Congo marks a decisive step towards the liberation of the whole African continent.

Your excellence, ladies and gentleman, my dear compatriots and my brothers in the struggle, this is what I want to tell you on behalf of the government on this magnificent day of our complete and sovereign independence.

Our government, strong, national, and popular, will be the salvation of the people.

Honor to the national freedom fighters!

Long live independence and African unity!

Long live the independent and sovereign Congo!

DOCUMENT 26

Mobutu Sese Seko on the world stage, 1983.[26]

In 1965, with backing from Belgium and the United States, a Congolese military officer named Joseph-Désiré Mobutu orchestrated a coup and took over control of the recently independent government of the Congo. During the 1970s he launched an Africanization campaign, changing the name of the country to Zaire and his own name to Mobutu Sese Seko. Throughout his rule Mobutu also plundered the country's economy and natural resources for his own gain, amassing a personal fortune estimated at five billion dollars. Mobutu's autocratic rule and economic exploitation of the Congo frequently invited comparisons with King Leopold. Backed by Western powers throughout the Cold War for his status as an anticommunist ally in Central Africa, Mobutu ruled the country for three decades. This account of a meeting with U.S. president Ronald Reagan illustrates the mutual support between Mobutu and the West. Note Reagan's emphasis on Mobutu's friendship and support for stability in Africa, both allusions to the Zairian president's anticommunist stance.

Remarks of President Reagan and President Mobutu Sese Seko of Zaire, August 4, 1983

President Reagan: President Mobutu and I have just had a warm and useful discussion. And I am pleased to have been able to meet again with President Mobutu, who's been a faithful friend to the United States for some 20 years. The President and I took this opportunity to review the state of U.S.–Zairian relations, and we found a large area of agreement on the major points we discussed.

I expressed our admiration for President Mobutu's courageous action in sending troops to assist the Government of Chad in its struggle against

---

26. Source: Ronald Reagan, "Remarks of President Reagan and President Mobutu Sese Seko of Zaire Following Their Meeting," August 4, 1983. Online by John Woolley and Gerhard Peters, *The American Presidency Project.* http://www.presidency.ucsb.edu/ws /index.php?pid=41671&st=Mobutu&st1=.

Libyan-backed rebels. On the home front, the President has informed me of progress on his government's economic stabilization plan. Zaire is taking the difficult but necessary steps to ensure sustained economic progress, and it's important that we and Zaire's other friends do what we can to help.

President Mobutu and I also discussed his country's political situation, and I told him of the positive reaction in the United States to his recent decision to offer amnesty to his political opponents.

This visit has permitted the President and me to reaffirm our common desire for peace and stability in Africa. And I am confident that the close relations between our two countries, based on shared interests and perceptions, will advance the cause of peace and development in Africa. And we're very pleased to have him visit us once again as he did a year and a half ago. Mr. President?

President Mobutu: I have expressed to President Reagan during our meeting, first of all, my thanks for the wonderful and warm welcome extended to us in the atmosphere of great friendship that we have experienced throughout our stay in Washington.

We surveyed world events. We talked about the economic situation in Zaire, about the program for financial and economic recovery which is being worked out with the IMF. We talked of Chad, of the aggression against that country, a founder of the OAU and a member of the United Nations. We talked also of Namibia, South Africa, and Central America. In brief, we surveyed world events. Some decisions have been made for economic aid to Zaire, and some more decisions will be made in that context.

I extended to President Reagan and to his associates my congratulations and thanks for all they have done to facilitate our stay in every way during our visit here. Thank you.

SELECT BIBLIOGRAPHY AND SUGGESTIONS FOR FURTHER READING

General Histories of Africa

The Cambridge History of Africa, 8 vols. Cambridge, UK: Cambridge University Press, 1975–86.

UNESCO General History of Africa, 8 vols. London: Heinemann, 1981–93.

Paul Bohannan and Philip Curtin. *Africa and Africans*, 4th ed. Long Grove, IL: Waveland Press, 1995.

Eric Gilbert and Jonathan T. Reynolds. *Africa in World History: From Prehistory to the Present*, 3rd ed. New York: Pearson, 2012.

John Iliffe. *Africans: The History of a Continent*, 2nd ed. Cambridge, UK: Cambridge University Press, 2007.

Richard J. Reid. *A History of Modern Africa, 1800 to the Present*. Oxford, UK: Wiley Blackwell, 2009.

Kevin Shillington. *History of Africa*, 3rd ed. New York: Palgrave/ Macmillan, 2012.

General Histories of Colonialism Before and During the "Scramble for Africa"

Albert Adu Boahen. *African Perspectives on Colonialism*. Baltimore, MD: Johns Hopkins University Press, 1989.

Muriel Evelyn Chamberlain. *The Scramble for Africa*, 3rd ed. London: Longman, 2010.

Stig Förster, Wolfgang Justin Mommsen, and Ronald Edward Robinson. *Bismarck, Europe and Africa: The Berlin West Africa Conference, 1884– 1885, and the Onset of Partition*. Oxford, UK: Oxford University Press, 1988.

Frank McLynn. *Hearts of Darkness: The European Exploration of Africa.* London: Basic Books, 1992.

David Northrup. *Africa's Discovery of Europe*, 3rd ed. New York: Oxford University Press, 2013.

Thomas Pakenham. *The Scramble for Africa 1876–1912.* New York: Random House, 1991.

Andrew Porter. *European Imperialism, 1860–1914.* London: Palgrave, 1994.

Henk L. Wesseling, translated by Arnold J. Pomerans. *Divide and Rule: The Partition of Africa, 1880–1914.* Westport, CT: Praeger, 1996.

Works on the Congo

Anne Hilton. *The Kingdom of Kongo.* Oxford, UK: Oxford University Press, 1985.

Adam Hochschild. *King Leopold's Ghost: A Story of Greed, Terror, and Heroism in Colonial Africa.* New York: Mariner Books, 1999.

Osumaka Likaka. *Naming Colonialism: History and Collective Memory in the Congo, 1870–1960.* Madison: University of Wisconsin Press, 2009.

Jules Marchal. *Lord Leverhulme's Ghosts: Colonial Exploitation in the Congo.* London: Verso, 2008.

Samuel H. Nelson. *Colonialism in the Congo Basin, 1880–1940.* Athens: Ohio University Press, 1994.

David Northrup. *Beyond the Bend in the River: African Labor in Eastern Zaire, 1865–1940.* Athens: Center for International Studies, University of Ohio, 1988.

Georges Nzongola-Ntalaja. *The Congo from Leopold to Kabila: A People's History.* London: Zed Books, 2002.

David Van Reybrouck, translated by Sam Garrett. *Congo: The Epic History of a People.* New York: Ecco Books, 2014.

Guy Vanthemsche. *Belgium and the Congo, 1885–1980.* New York: Cambridge University Press, 2012.

Michela Wrong. *In the Footsteps of Mr. Kurtz: Living on the Brink of Disaster in Mobutu's Congo.* London: 4th Estate, 2000.

Works on Key Historical Figures

Heinrich Brode, translated by H. Havelock. *Tippu Tip: The Story of His Career in Zanzibar and Central Africa*. Zanzibar: Gallery Publications, 2000.

Barbara Emerson. *Leopold II of the Belgians: King of Colonialism*. London: St. Martin's Press, 1979.

Leda Farrant. *Tippu Tip and the East African Slave Trade*. London: Hamish Hamilton, 1975.

John Hope Franklin. *George Washington Williams: A Biography*. Chicago: University of Chicago Press, 1985.

Brian Inglis. *Roger Casement*. London: Hodder & Stodden, 1973.

Tim Jeal. *Stanley: The Impossible Life of Africa's Greatest Explorer*. London: Faber and Faber, 2007.

Pamela Newkirk. *Spectacle: The Astonishing Life of Ota Benga*. London: HarperCollins, 2015.

Roger Sawyer. *Casement: The Flawed Hero*. London: Routledge, 1984.

INDEX